IN NO TIME

Word
97

IN NO TIME

Word 97

Walter Schwabe

Edited by
ROB YOUNG

 **Prentice Hall Europe**

London New York Toronto Sydney Tokyo Singapore Madrid Mexico City Munich Paris

First published in 1997 as Easy – Word 97 by
Markt&Technik Buch- und Software Verlag GmbH
85540 Haar bei München/Germany
This edition published 1999 by
Prentice Hall Europe
Campus 400, Maylands Avenue
Hemel Hempstead
Hertfordshire, HP2 7EZ

A division of
Simon & Schuster International Group

Translated by Lilian Hall and Harriet Horsfield
in association with First Edition Translations Limited, Cambridge

Typeset in Stone Sans
by Mike Weintroub

Designed and Produced by Bender Richardson White

Printed and bound in Great Britain
by T J International, Padstow, Cornwall

Library of Congress Cataloging-in-Publication Data

Available from the publisher

British Library Cataloguing in Publication Data

A catalogue record for this book is available from the British Library

ISBN 0-13-977653-2

1   2   3   4   5   03   02   01   00   99

Contents

Inventory

Valuables	Receipt No.	Date	Amount in £
Stereo system	1	20.04.95	495.00
Television	2	23.12.95	425.00
Gold necklace	3	31.02.96	300.00
Computer	4	02.01.97	970.00
Washing machine	5	10.01.97	300.00
Gold ring	6	20.09.97	833.00
Watch	7	21.09.97	1500.99
Total valuables:			5023.99

Dear Sir or Madam

I would like to order the following items from you

Item No.	Item	Quantity
00001	Trousers, grey	50
4711	Blouse, red	50
0897	Socks, red	120
007	T-shirt, yellow	200
008	T-shirt, blue	400
009	T-shirt, black	100
1010	Pullover, yellow	10

Yours faithfully,

Charles Benson 7 Drovers Lane Sawby SY12 3PT

Mr Harold Benson
815 Park Drive
Sawby SY1 2BA

Invoice No: 07/1001

Dear Mr Benson

Thank you for you order. Our invoice is below for your kind attention.

Item	Order	Unit Price	Quantity	Total Price in £
1	Table, Paradise	600 *	2	1200
2	Desk, Senator	1000 *	2	2000
		Total		3200
		VAT * 0.175		560
		Amount owing		3760

Dear reader,

By buying this book you have opted for a somewhat different method of learning. Anyone who has passed their driving test will recognise the problem: the theory is boring, driving becomes fun and easy only with hands-on practice on the road. In No Time is guided by this principle too. A wealth of examples will help you get to know Word step by step. The first objective is to overcome the beginner's instinctive fear of anything new. The chapters are arranged so that you can even make a hands-on start with Word (e.g. writing out bills or greetings cards, drawing up inventories etc.). I cannot stress enough how important it is to do the exercises. They will not only consolidate your knowledge, but will also show you other ways of doing things.

Finally, I would like to thank those people who attended my Word for Beginners courses. Not only did they show me the problems which beginners face, but they also motivated me to write this book. I would particularly like to thank the older members of my classes, who did not have a clue beforehand, thought a mouse was just vermin but became increasingly enthusiastic about Word as the course progressed.

I am sure that you, the reader, will soon have just as much fun with Word as my 'guinea-pigs'. And by the end of the book you too will definitely be saying, 'Word - it really is quite EASY!'

On another note, if you find you enjoy Word and would also like to learn Excel 97, I can recommend Excel In No Time.

Regards

Walter Schwabe

The following three pages show the layout of your computer keyboard. For the sake of clarity, only specific blocks of keys are introduced at any one time. Many of the computer keys function in the same way as typewriter keys. But there are also some additional keys which are geared to particular features of computer work, as you will discover for yourself...

Typewriter keyboard

You use these keys just as you would on a typewriter.
You also use the Enter key to send commands to the computer.

Tab key

Caps lock

Backspace

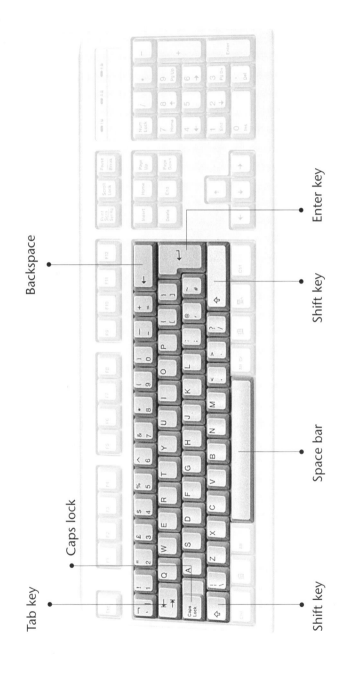

Enter key

Shift key

Space bar

Shift key

Special keys, function keys, control lights, number pad

Special keys and function keys are used for particular tasks in computing. `Ctrl`, `Alt` and `Alt Gr` are mostly used in combination with other keys. You can use the `Esc` key to stop commands; the Insert and Delete keys can be used to insert or delete text, for example.

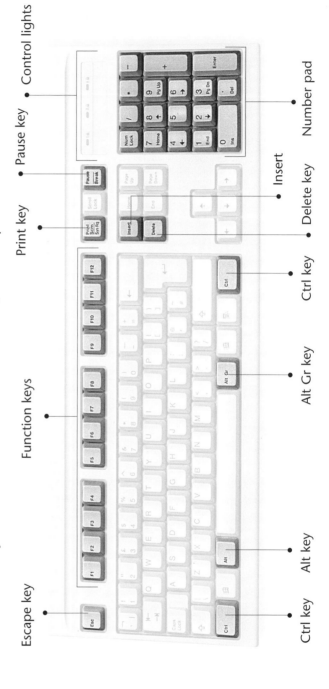

Escape key

Function keys

Print key

Pause key • Control lights

Ctrl key   Alt key

Alt Gr key

Ctrl key

Insert

• Delete key   Number pad

Navigation keys

You use these keys to move about the screen.

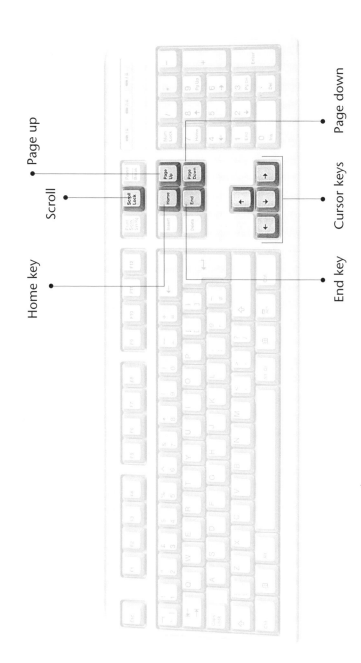

Home key

Scroll

Page up

Page down

Cursor keys

End key

'Click ...'

This means quickly press
a button once.

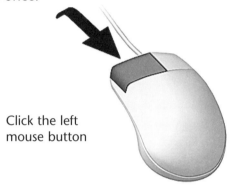

Click the left
mouse button

Click the right
mouse button

'Double-click ...'

This means briefly press
the left button twice
in quick succession.

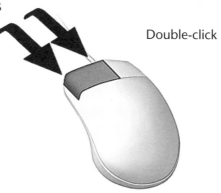

Double-click

'Drag ...'

This means using the left mouse button,
click on a particular item on the screen,
hold the button down, move the mouse
and then drag the item to a different
position.

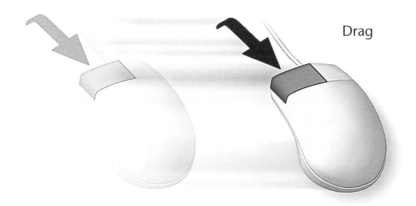

Drag

17

What's in this chapter?

There is always a first time in life. You look at your monitor and suddenly see a completely unknown world before you. Just remember, we were all beginners once. Maybe, right now, if someone were to ask you 'What is Word?', you would be totally at a loss for an answer. In this first chapter, as well as learning how to start Word 97, you will also get to know the basics of moving around the program. How is the screen laid out and what do all the 'buttons' and 'grey areas' mean?

The first time Word 97

In No Time

You are going to learn:

19

Starting Word

To be able to carry out word processing work once the program has been successfully installed, you must first bring Word 97 up again. But that's obvious, you will be thinking. And indeed it is! Except that, with Word, there are several ways of doing this. Later, when you have filed (i.e. saved) letters and documents, you will have even more alternatives. Which should you choose? It's purely a matter of opinion. Here are two alternatives to choose from. You will find more information on installation in the chapter on Word Help.

The first way

Word 97 is a word-processing program. You can bring up many programs in Windows 97 using the Start menu. You will usually find the button for this menu at the bottom of your monitor screen.

 Click the left mouse button on the Start button and select the Programs entry in the Start menu.

A second menu is now opened, in which, once installed, Word 97 appears with its own icon. To start the program, click once on the Word icon.

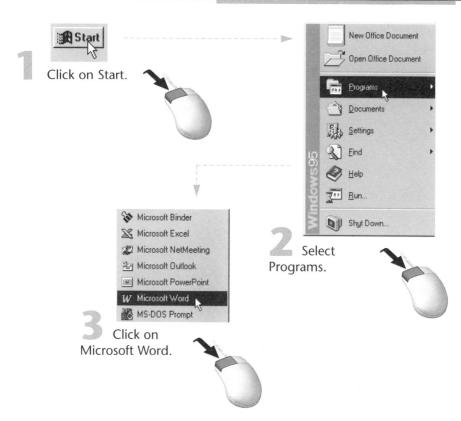

1 Click on Start.

2 Select Programs.

3 Click on Microsoft Word.

The second way

When starting Word the second way, you must again first open the Start menu. Here you will find the New Office Document button.

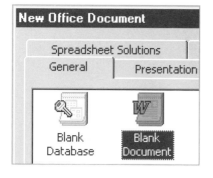

What is a dialog box?

A new window (also known as a dialog box) is displayed. You will find the name right at the top: New Office Document. You will often be working with such input windows with Word.

21

What are tabs?

Spreadsheet Solutions	Presentations	Web Pages	Binders	Databases
General	Presentation Designs	Letters & Faxes	Memos	Other Documents

Dialog boxes often have many tabs. This is like working with a card index. In our example, you need the General tab. Instead of flicking through, simply click the mouse button on the name of the page you require. This will automatically appear in the foreground. You will come across tabs even more often when working with Word later on.

Now you can activate the Blank document entry either by double-clicking the mouse or by selecting it (clicking it once) using the left mouse button and

then clicking OK to confirm. Either way, the result is the same: Word 97 starts and appears on your screen together with a blank document.

1 Click on Start.

2 Select the New Office Document entry.

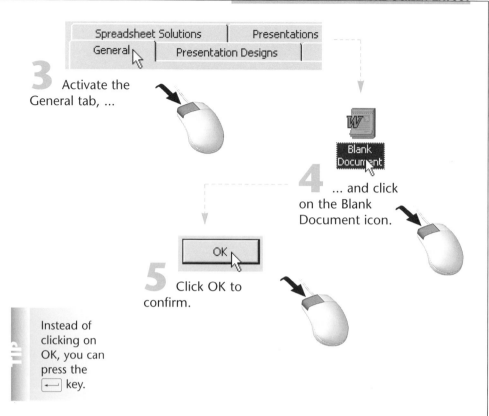

3 Activate the General tab, ...

4 ... and click on the Blank Document icon.

5 Click OK to confirm.

Instead of clicking on OK, you can press the ⮐ key.

The screen layout

When Word 97 is started for the first time, a lively Assistant immediately introduces himself. This is Clipit. He will help you work with Word 97 and can be very useful, but occasionally he can also be a trouble-maker. We will be dealing with this cheerful, oddball character later, so switch him off for now. All you have to do is to click the left mouse button on the cross and he will disappear from the screen.

When the program has been started, what is known as Word 97's user interface is displayed on the screen.

Command zone

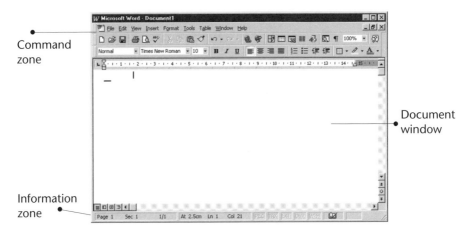

Document window

Information zone

Put simply, the user interface is what you see on the screen when using Word 97.

You will enter your text in the white area later. The text will appear where the dash (called the cursor, also known as the insertion point indicator) is flashing.

The end-of-document indicator is very important: it shows that your text (also known as a document) is definitely finished at this point. If we were using a typewriter, the end-of-document indicator would be the end of an inserted sheet of paper.

The insertion point indicator is a position marker on the screen in the form of a flashing dash. It indicates the place where the next text to be inserted will appear.

The screen is divided into three zones:

At the top, there is the command zone. As its name suggests, this is where commands are given and carried out using the mouse or the keyboard. The second (white) area is the document window for entering text.

If you click the mouse in the command zone, you cannot continue writing in the document window. Just click the mouse pointer in the document window and you will cancel the command zone again.

The third is the information zone. It is at the bottom of the screen.

Different mouse pointers

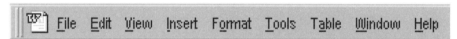

The mouse pointer shows you exactly where you are. It looks different depending on its position on the screen. If it is in the command or information zone, the mouse pointer will be shown as an arrow.

$\boxed{\text{I}}$ If, on the other hand, you position the mouse pointer in the document window, it appears as an I-beam, as shown here in the margin.

The command zone

You will find several different bars in the command zone:

The title and document bar

W Microsoft Word - Document1 This always shows what document (i.e. letter, text) you are in at the moment. The word 'Document' means that this document has not been saved yet. It is a name which Word 97 gives automatically. (The 'Save' function will be explained in a later chapter.) The '1' after 'Document' means that you are working on your first new document on the screen at the moment.

The menu bar

| W | File | Edit | View | Insert | Format | Tools | Table | Window | Help |

The commands (e.g. Save, Print, Close) are carried out on the menu bar if you click the mouse on them. It is called a 'menu' because a selection can be made here, just as it can from a restaurant menu.

You can also get into the menu bar using the keyboard:

Function	**Keyboard shortcut**

You can also get into the menu bar by using these keys. (Tip: First press and release the [Alt] , then press the [→] key.)

[Alt] and [→]

You can move around more in the menu bar using the cursor keys.

   [←]

Use the [Esc] key to exit the menu bar again.

CAUTION

Never try to write when you are in the command zone, as you will unintentionally give a command. The underlined letters in the menu mean that when the appropriate key is pressed, Word carries out this command. If you want to type the word 'fame', for example, when the first two letters 'fa' are entered, the command Files/Save As... is carried out (if it is the command area which is activated and not the document window).

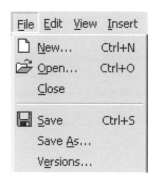

The standard toolbar

WHAT'S THIS?

An icon - which simply means a 'little picture' - is a symbolic representation on the screen (for example, the outline of a printer to denote printing) which can represent a function.

The standard toolbar contains what are known as icons or buttons. They symbolise frequently-used commands, which you can also carry out by using the menu bar. The advantage of the standard toolbar over the menu bar is that you can control the individual commands more quickly using the mouse.

The formatting toolbar

TIP

All commands on the menu bar, standard and formatting toolbars are carried out by simply clicking the left mouse button.

This toolbar enables you to 'format' documents. This means that you can select a different font, for example, emphasise your text in bold or underline it.

The ruler

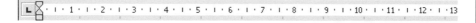

The ruler is like a measuring tape. You will learn how to use it later (e.g. setting tabs).

27

The information zone

Here you will find the status bar. It tells you exactly where you are in the document. Position the cursor in the top left corner of your document. The status bar will show you all the information you need to know at that particular moment.

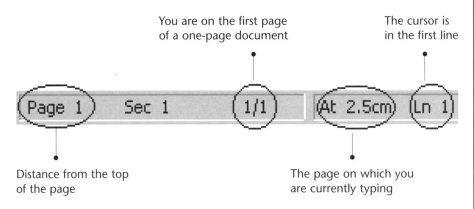

You are on the first page
of a one-page document

The cursor is
in the first line

Distance from the top
of the page

The page on which you
are currently typing

Switching the individual bars on and off

In Word 97 you can switch the individual bars on and off at any time. To do this, you always use the View menu.

Switching off the ruler

Clicking on View on the menu bar opens the appropriate menu. Now you can switch the ruler on and off. A tick in front of it means it is already activated. Click the left mouse button on the tick to switch the ruler on (with tick) or off (no tick) on your screen.

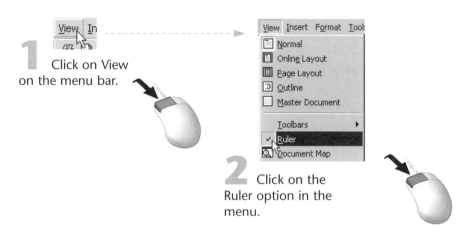

1 Click on View on the menu bar.

2 Click on the Ruler option in the menu.

Switching off the standard and formatting toolbars

Select the Toolbars option in the View menu. This will open a drop-down menu listing all the toolbars available in Word 97. There should be a tick in front of Standard and Formatting. This means that they are activated. If you now click on one of the ticks, the respective bar will be switched off on your screen. The individual bars can be switched on again in the same way.

> A tick in front of a toolbar means that it is activated (switched on).

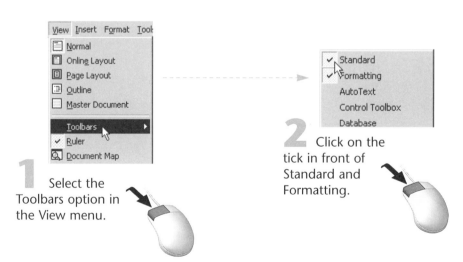

1 Select the Toolbars option in the View menu.

2 Click on the tick in front of Standard and Formatting.

29

Moving the individual bars

The inexperienced beginner is often faced with the apparently insoluble problem of the toolbars having moved. This usually happens when the computer is also being used by other people. The best thing to do is to learn for yourself how to move the bars. Then you can customise your working area. When a bar is going to be moved, you will see a broken line around it. You can move this around the screen by pressing on the mouse button. In this way, a toolbar can be dragged into the working area to give a better and quicker view of the text. Dragging is just a matter of practice. Customise your screen to get it just how you want it. Using the same method, you can of course return the toolbar to its original position.

1 Click on the ridged area of the Standard toolbar, keeping the left mouse button pressed down.

2 With the mouse button still pressed down, drag the standard toolbar ...

3 ... to the desired position, then release the mouse button.

Animations

Word 97 offers an optical effect with the Animations function. You can use this to format individual menu options. Select one of the animations in the Options tab.

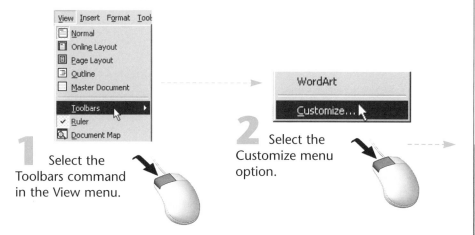

1 Select the Toolbars command in the View menu.

2 Select the Customize menu option.

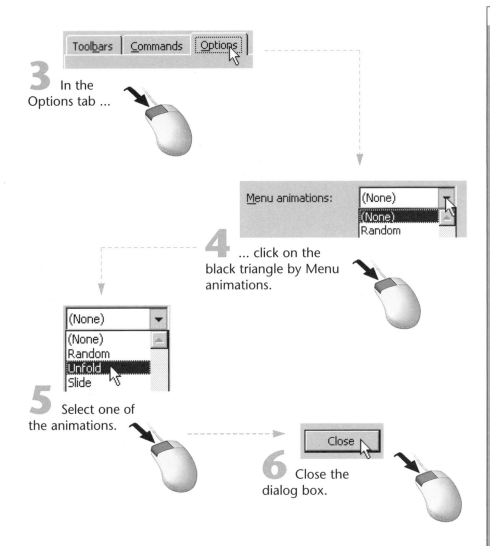

3 In the Options tab ...

4 ... click on the black triangle by Menu animations.

5 Select one of the animations.

6 Close the dialog box.

Depicting the animations

When you subsequently open any menu, you will see your selected animation. Unfortunately we cannot show these in this book. If you do not wish to use menu animations, then simply opt for the (None) entry in the list.

ScreenTips

Word will help you to get to know the individual icons in the standard and formatting toolbars better. Position the mouse pointer on any icon. After a short time you will be shown a ScreenTip. This will give you a tip about the command that the icon represents. The information in brackets

It is advisable to have the ScreenTip option switched on until you are familiar with Word 97. The tips make it much easier to get to grips with Word 97!

means that, alternatively, you can press this combination of keys to give the command. (Tip: in this example, you must first press and hold down the Ctrl-key, then type the letter O.)

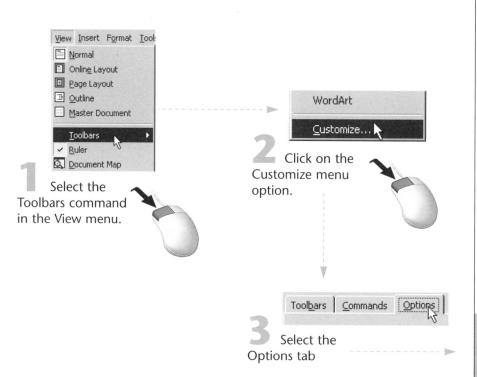

1 Select the Toolbars command in the View menu.

2 Click on the Customize menu option.

3 Select the Options tab

☑ Show ScreenTips on toolbars
☑ Show shortcut keys in ScreenTips

4 Click on the white boxes by both options

5 Close the dialog box.

An Option changes the Word 97 settings. These come into effect as soon as you click on a different tab or close the dialog box.

As soon as you have clicked, a tick appears in both boxes (also called checkboxes). The options are now activated. Without pressing either button, place the mouse pointer on any icon. The ScreenTips facility is now switched on.

The Zoom function

You can enlarge or reduce the text on your screen with the help of Zoom. It is important to note that this function does not alter the font size when it comes to printing out, but serves only to give a better picture on the monitor. Imagine it like the zoom lens in a camera or a pair of binoculars. You can indeed make the subjects appear closer, but the actual size of the subject is not changed.

Now type in the example text 'The first text'. We will use it to demonstrate the Zoom function.

The first way of setting the Zoom

You can adjust the Zoom setting right on your screen. To do this, click on the standard toolbar box showing the percentage (ScreenTip: 'Zoom'), and key in any number using the keyboard. Then press the ⬅ key. There is no need to enter the percentage sign (%) too. Word adds this automatically.

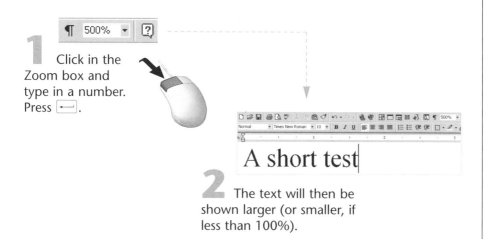

1 Click in the Zoom box and type in a number. Press ⬅.

2 The text will then be shown larger (or smaller, if less than 100%).

A short test

The second way of setting the Zoom

A drop-down menu will appear only when you click on the icon with the inverted triangle. Then select any item from the list shown.

Another way of setting the Zoom is as follows: click on the small black triangle; this opens the drop-down menu and you can click on the desired Zoom factor in the option list.

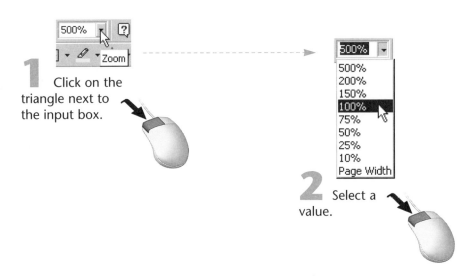

1 Click on the triangle next to the input box.

2 Select a value.

The third way of setting the Zoom

Select the Zoom command in the View menu and click on the desired Zoom option. You can set your individual zoom factor in the Percent box.

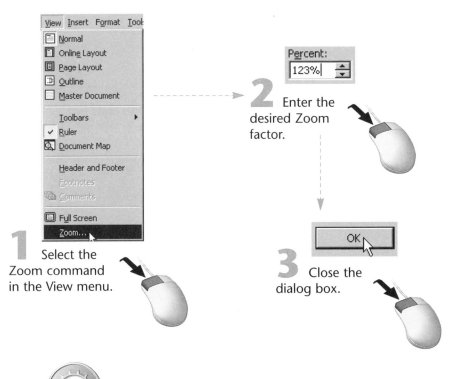

1 Select the Zoom command in the View menu.

2 Enter the desired Zoom factor.

3 Close the dialog box.

Closing Word without saving

Do you want to finish your work with Word 97? As you have not entered anything of importance, nothing needs to be saved. Saving means that you could carry on working on the saved text/document when you next start up Word 97.

Closing the program

When you bring up the Exit command, and you have not yet saved the text you have already entered, Word will point this out to you and ask if you would like to save your text. As you do not need to save it at the moment, answer this question with No. If you were to click on the Cancel button, you would return to the text, just as if nothing had happened.

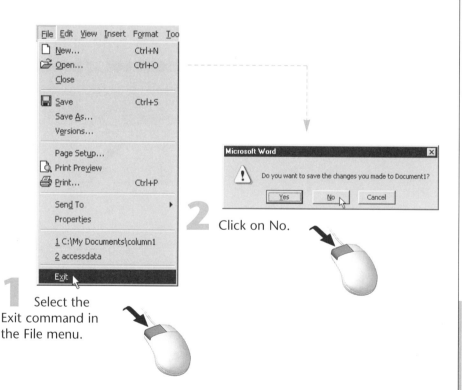

Click on No.

Select the Exit command in the File menu.

Using the mouse to close

Another way is to close Word using the mouse. To do this, double-click on the large blue W in the title bar or activate the cross in the top right corner by clicking just once with the mouse. Again, you will be asked whether you wish to save the text. If you answer No, you will exit the program altogether.

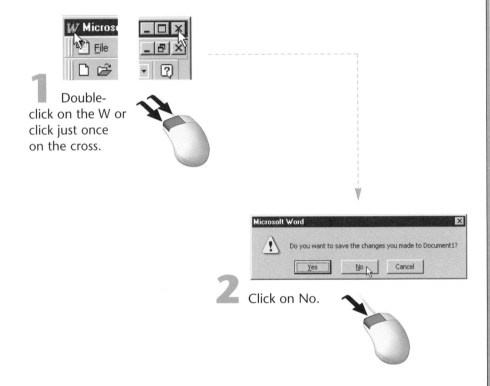

1 Double-click on the W or click just once on the cross.

2 Click on No.

The Word Trainer

Practice makes perfect! The more you practise, the deeper and broader your knowledge of Word will become.

Exercise 1
Which toolbars can you see in the picture below?

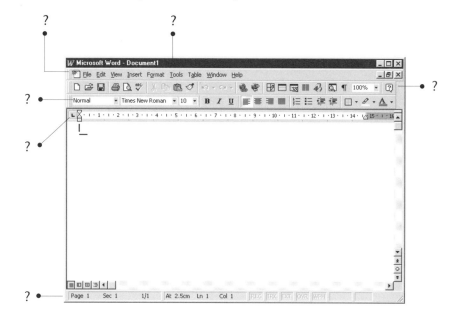

Exercise 2

Carry out the following tasks using Word 97:

➡ Deactivate the ruler.

➡ Set the Zoom to 121 %.

➡ Deactivate the standard toolbar.

➡ Switch off the formatting toolbar.

➡ Switch on again the ruler and the standard formatting toolbar.

Exercise 3

Answer the following questions (only one answer is correct):

☞ With which of the following keys can you activate the menu bar?

⌨ ⟵

⌨ Alt

⌨ Alt Gr

⌨ Ctrl

☞ Which command sequence would you use to switch on the ScreenTips?

Format/Draw/ScreenTips

View/Toolbars/Customize/ScreenTips tab

View/Toolbars/Customize/Options tab/Display ScreenTips on toolbars

☞ What does your mouse pointer look like when it is in the document window?

☞ What is the purpose of the end-of-document indicator?

Any text entered will appear where the end-of-document indicator is situated.

The document ends at that point.

Marks the end of a sentence.

The sy-lla-ble ri-ddle

Use the syllables to form the correct answers. Four syllables will be left over to give the answer to the riddle.

Syllables: sta-text-pro-zoom-ker-mouse-tips-end-op-tus-view-mar-tabs-word-bar-screen-cess-tions-of-ing-

---

You will find information here, e.g. which page of the document you are on at the moment.

Indicator and input device Shows the end of a document

You use the .... menu to activate the ruler.

If the mouse pointer stays on an icon for more than a second, the explanation of that icon appears.

You use this to enlarge or reduce the view of your document.

You switch on the ScreenTips by the View/Toolbars command, choosing Customize from the toolbar submenu, then clicking on the .... tab to reveal the checkbox.

They have 'index labels' (with the appropriate name on) which are used to bring them to the front.

The answer to the riddle is: _____

Did you get them all right?

Then go on to the next chapter!

What's in this chapter?

And now we're off: you are going to write your first letter. And so that the reader does not overlook certain words, such as a meeting place or time, for example, you are going to emphasise them. Since everyone makes mistakes, Word gives you practical help with spelling. You are going to save your text, which is just like filing a document away in a folder. All you need to do then is print it out, put it in an envelope and pop it in the post!

John Harris
12 Highlands Lane
Ashington AT1 2TZ

Angela Williamson
37 Pine Road
Grandholme GH2 7DP

Invitation

Dear Ms Williamson

My wife and I have recently opened a new garden furniture shop at **44 Lime Avenue**. As one of our most valued customers, we would like to invite you to a *Grand Opening Party* on 29.2.99 at 20.00.

With kind regards,

Nonprinting characters

 When you have started Word up again, key in the first text. A button in the standard toolbar will enable you to see what are known as 'nonprinting' characters. You are going to find out about these now.

When is a full stop not a full stop?

When you have typed in a few words, you will suddenly see little dots between the words. These are in no way related to the

| John·Harris |

'ordinary' full stop (.). They will not be printed out later, but are shown only on the screen (hence the name 'nonprinting characters'). In our example we used the space bar to make a space between the words 'John' and 'Harris'.

| John Harris |

The advantage of the nonprinting characters is that you can see exactly what has been done in the text. For example: without this

| John··Harris¶ |

function, it is hard to spot it immediately if you have inserted two spaces by mistake.

| ris¶ | When you press the ⌐ key, you will move on to the next line. This rather odd-looking character will be shown on the screen.

Experience shows that beginners find it difficult to get used to the nonprinting characters. But do leave them activated. Then you will always be able to see which keys you have pressed. In the following pages of this book these characters will enable you to understand exactly what you have to do. In this way, you will see from the pictures exactly when you must press the ⌐ key or [Space], for example.

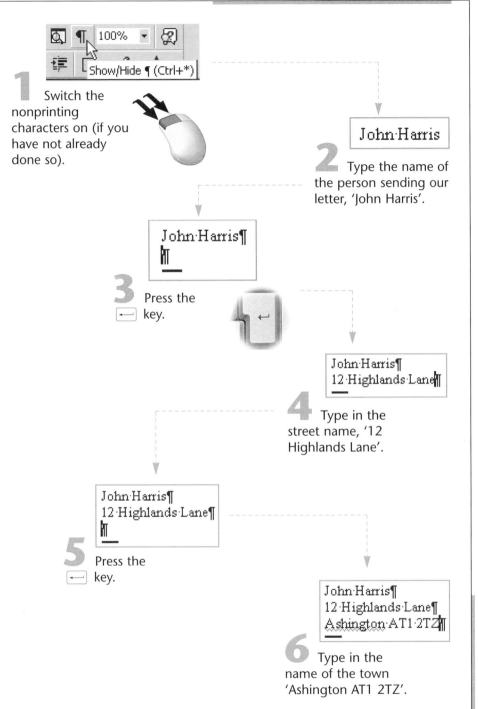

1 Switch the nonprinting characters on (if you have not already done so).

Show/Hide ¶ (Ctrl+*)

2 Type the name of the person sending our letter, 'John Harris'.

John·Harris

John·Harris¶

3 Press the ⏎ key.

John·Harris¶
12·Highlands·Lane¶

4 Type in the street name, '12 Highlands Lane'.

John·Harris¶
12·Highlands·Lane¶

5 Press the ⏎ key.

John·Harris¶
12·Highlands·Lane¶
Ashington·AT1·2TZ¶

6 Type in the name of the town 'Ashington AT1 2TZ'.

45

The spell checker

'It'a onsy humab tp mske mistales!' With Word, spelling can be checked during or after input.

Unknown phrases

In our example, one of the things Word objects to as soon as you use the ⎡Space⎤ or ⎡←⎤ key is the place name 'Ashington'. The word

is highlighted by a wavy, red line. Of course, this line will not be printed, but serves only to indicate that Word finds this term wrong.

But 'Ashington' is in fact written correctly. The software queries the term because it is a proper noun and is unknown. Move the mouse pointer onto the word and click on it with the right mouse button. This opens the spell checker's shortcut menu, in which Word gives you some correction suggestions. But we do not accept these, as 'Ashington' is in fact written correctly. You have a choice between Ignore All and Add. By choosing the first option, you tell Word that the word 'Ashington' is correct and Word should no longer 'find fault with it' in this letter (this document). By choosing Add, you indicate that in future, Word should always recognise 'Ashington' as being correct. This means that it does not just apply for this letter, but also for all other documents you may write in the future.

Information

While you are typing, you will see in the status bar below, that Word is constantly checking spelling.

Word will tell you if a mistake is found.

The program will also show you if you have corrected a mistake.

Switching off the lines

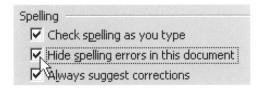

If the wavy red lines get on your nerves, you can switch them off. To do this, select the Tools/Options menu command and simply switch off the function in the Spelling and Grammar tab by activating the Hide spelling errors in this document checkbox. In this tab, you can also choose whether Word should check the spelling as you type or leave you to check the spelling when the document is complete. Removing the checkmark from this box will also remove those wavy lines.

Checking the completed document

If you prefer to run a spell check when the document is finished, click on the standard toolbar icon shown in the margin, press the [F7] function key or choose the Spelling and Grammar command in the Tools menu.

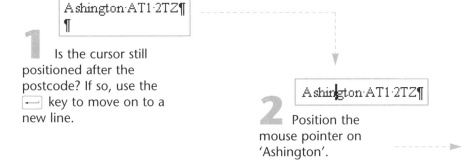

1 Is the cursor still positioned after the postcode? If so, use the [←] key to move on to a new line.

2 Position the mouse pointer on 'Ashington'.

47

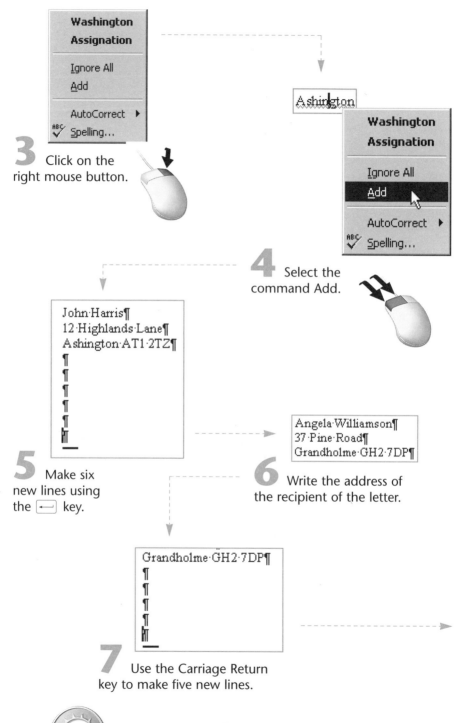

Washington
Assignation

Ignore All
Add

AutoCorrect ▶
Spelling...

3 Click on the
right mouse button.

Ashington

Washington
Assignation

Ignore All
Add

AutoCorrect ▶
Spelling...

4 Select the
command Add.

John·Harris¶
12·Highlands·Lane¶
Ashington·AT1·2TZ¶
¶
¶
¶
¶
¶
¶

5 Make six
new lines using
the ← key.

Angela·Williamson¶
37·Pine·Road¶
Grandholme·GH2·7DP¶

6 Write the address of
the recipient of the letter.

Grandholme·GH2·7DP¶
¶
¶
¶
¶
¶

7 Use the Carriage Return
key to make five new lines.

8 Deliberately key in the word 'Invitation' wrong as 'Invidation'.

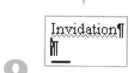

9 Move on to a new line using the [←] key.

Correcting mistakes

Of course, everybody writes words incorrectly sometimes. And if you do, Word will offer you some suggested solutions, which you can accept.

1 Position the mouse pointer on the incorrect word 'Invidation'.

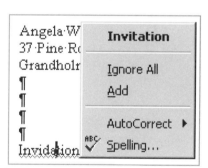

2 Click on the right mouse button.

49

Invidation¶

| Invitation |
| Ignore All |
| Add |
| AutoCorrect ▶ |
| ABC Spelling... |

3 Select the correction suggestion Invitation.

Invitation¶
¶
¶
Dear Ms Williamson¶
¶
My wife and I have recently opened a new garden furniture shop at 44 Lime Avenue. As one of our most valued customers, we would like to invite you to a Grand Opening Party on 29.2.99 at 20.00.¶
¶
With kind regards,¶
¶
¶
¶
John Harris¶

4 Make three new lines using the ⟵ key and key in the full text of the letter:

"Dear Ms Williamson

My wife and I have recently opened a new garden furniture shop at 44 Lime Avenue. As one of our most valued customers, we would like to invite you to a Grand Opening Party on 29.2.99 at 20.00.

With kind regards,

John Harris"

Aligning lines

In Word, lines can be aligned in various ways. Thus lines can be left-aligned, right-aligned or centre-aligned. You usually write from left to right. To emphasise the subject of our letter, we can show it centred above the main part of the text. To do this, the cursor must be in the appropriate line, i.e. the cursor is flashing in this line. Right alignment is often used in tables.

Another button on the formatting toolbar, shown to the left, is known as Justify. This means that the lines are aligned between the left and right margin so that they fit exactly into the text area and in this way an 'unjustified edge' is avoided.

Yesterday I went for a walk in a dark wood. Suddenly a UFO landed right before my eyes. The door opened and a fair-haired monster wearing black sunglasses came up to me. The unknown being greeted me by saying, in a piercing voice, "Dark brown is the hazelnut, dark brown am I too, am I too...". It was terrible. Never in my entire life had I heard anything quite so terrifying.

Yesterday I went for a walk in a dark wood. Suddenly a UFO landed right before my eyes. The door opened and a fair-haired monster wearing black sunglasses came up to me. The unknown being greeted me by saying, in a piercing voice, "Dark brown is the hazelnut, dark brown am I too, am I too...". It was terrible. Never in my entire life had I heard anything quite so terrifying.

In Word, you can also set line spacing. Press and hold the Ctrl key, and type a figure (such as 2 for double-spaced text).

You will often find justification used in books, newspapers and magazines. A disadvantage of justification is that unsightly large gaps can appear between words, especially where lines are short.

Keyboard shortcuts	Function
Ctrl + 1	Single-line spacing
Ctrl + 2	Double-line spacing
Ctrl + 3	One-and-a-half line spacing

51

1 Click on the line containing the word 'Invitation'.

Center (Ctrl+E)

2 Click the Center icon on the formatting toolbar.

Emphasising text

You can format text in different ways, by emphasising it in bold or italic, or underlining it. Text which has been formatted in this way stands out more to the reader. Text can also be emphasised by changing the font and font size. In Word, these processes are called formatting. You will therefore find the appropriate tools on the formatting toolbar.

> **TIP**
> A tick in front of a toolbar means that it is activated (switched on).

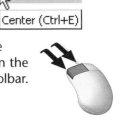

1 Click on the word 'Invitation'?

Times New Roman ▼ 10 ▼

2 Click on the little triangle-button next to Font.

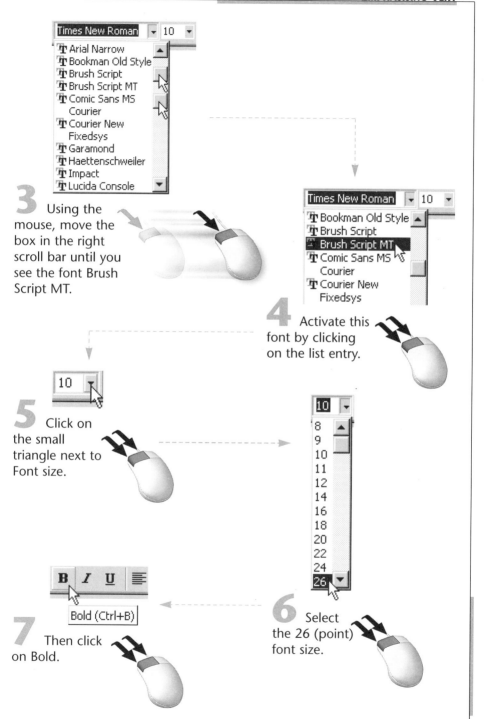

3 Using the mouse, move the box in the right scroll bar until you see the font Brush Script MT.

4 Activate this font by clicking on the list entry.

5 Click on the small triangle next to Font size.

6 Select the 26 (point) font size.

7 Then click on Bold.

Bold (Ctrl+B)

Emphasising a word

If you wish to format a single word or term, it is often quite sufficient to place the cursor on it and click. In Word, a word always stretches from one space to the next. In our example, we are going to use italics: a font which leans slightly to the right.

Grand·Opening·Party

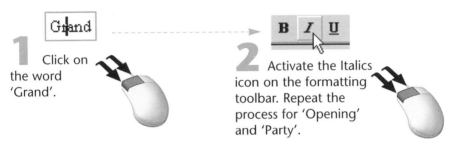

1 Click on the word 'Grand'.

2 Activate the Italics icon on the formatting toolbar. Repeat the process for 'Opening' and 'Party'.

Selecting

If you wish to emphasise several words or a phrase, you select it – in this case, the house number and the street.

44·Lime·Avenue

44·Lime·Avenue There are several ways of select text. Using the mouse is definitely the quickest way. Place the mouse pointer in front of the word, hold down the left mouse button and drag the cursor over the phrases that you want to select. If you still have difficulties using the mouse, you can also fall back on the keyboard. Again, position the cursor in front of the terms to be selected, press the [⇧] key, hold it down and move the [→] key along until you reach the end of the area you want to select.

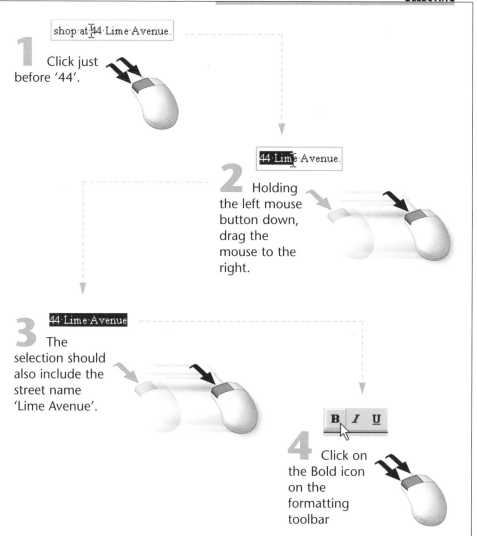

shop·at·44·Lime·Avenue.

1 Click just before '44'.

44·Lim e·Avenue.

2 Holding the left mouse button down, drag the mouse to the right.

44·Lime·Avenue

3 The selection should also include the street name 'Lime Avenue'.

B *I* U

4 Click on the Bold icon on the formatting toolbar

Quick selection using the mouse

It is often quicker to select drawings, areas of text or whole documents using the mouse. You just need to know how to do it!

55

Selection	Mouse action
Word	Place mouse pointer on word and double-click.
Line	Move the pointer to the left of the line until the arrow points upwards towards the right. Then click.
Several lines	As for a line, hold the mouse button down and drag up or down.
Sentence	Hold `Ctrl` and click the left mouse button on the sentence.
Large area of text	Click at the position where the selection should start, keep the `ⓞ` key pressed and click at the position where you wish the selection to stop.
Entire text	An alternative to using the menu command Edit/Select All: position the mouse pointer before the beginning of the text (the arrow will point upwards towards the right), keep the `Ctrl` key pressed down and click.

Deleting selections

You can get rid of selections again by clicking anywhere in the text.

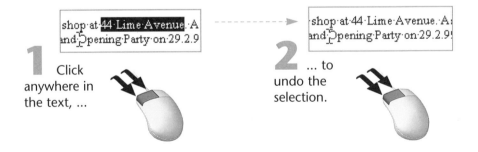

1 Click anywhere in the text, ...

2 ... to undo the selection.

Formatting

Removing formatting

A format (highlight) can be removed by clicking on the word, or selecting the text in question and then reactivating the format which it is intended to delete.

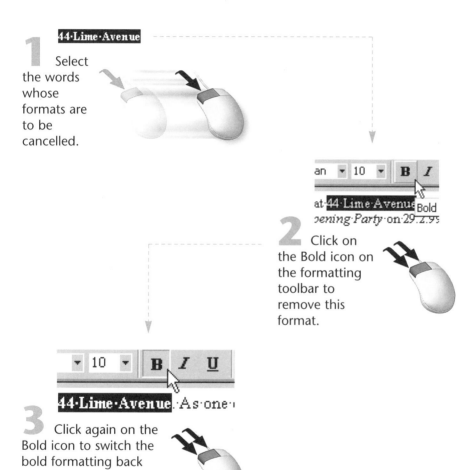

1 Select the words whose formats are to be cancelled.

2 Click on the Bold icon on the formatting toolbar to remove this format.

3 Click again on the Bold icon to switch the bold formatting back on again.

Other formatting styles

As well as Bold, Italics and Underlining, you will find even more ways to create effects in the Format/Font menu option. To do this, you use the Font tab. Here you can also double-underline words or put characters in superscript or subscript.

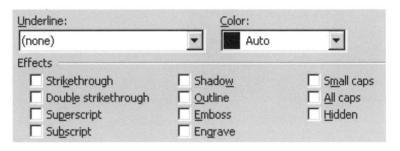

In our letter, we would like to double-underline the date '29.2.99'

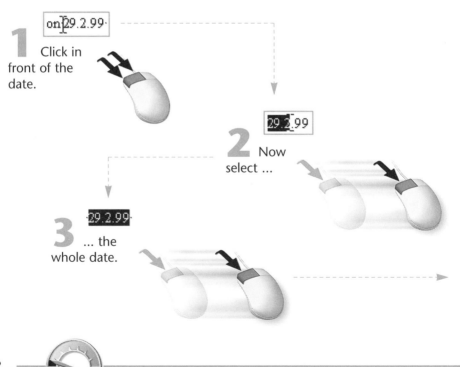

1 Click in front of the date.

on 29.2.99

2 Now select ...

29.2.99

3 ... the whole date.

29.2.99

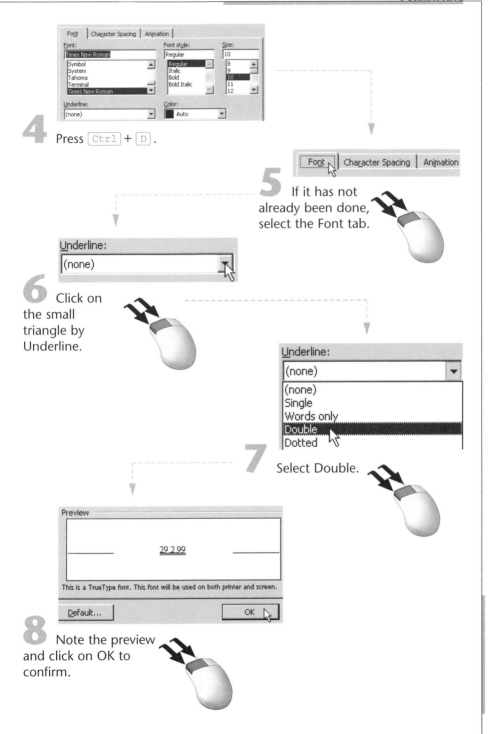

4 Press Ctrl + D.

5 If it has not already been done, select the Font tab.

6 Click on the small triangle by Underline.

7 Select Double.

8 Note the preview and click on OK to confirm.

59

Formatting with keys

You can carry out formatting such as Bold, Italic, Underlining etc. by using the formatting toolbar or by selecting the Format/Font menu option. Alternatively, you can achieve the same effect using key combinations (also called 'keyboard shortcuts'). Here is a summary:

Format keyboard shortcuts

Format	Keyboard Shortcut
Bold	Ctrl + B
Italics	Ctrl + I
Superscript	Ctrl + ⇧ + =
Subscript	Ctrl + =
Small capitals	Ctrl + ⇧ + K
Block capitals	Ctrl + ⇧ + A
Underlining	Ctrl + U
Double underlining	Ctrl + ⇧ + D

Superscript

Back to the text. When stating the time, 20.00, the last two noughts – i.e. the minutes – should be underlined and in superscript.

at·20.⁰⁰

You can put characters into superscript by using either the Font tab from the Format/Font menu option or the keyboard shortcut Ctrl + ⇧ + = (see summary).

As already mentioned, formatting can be applied whilst the text is being typed or afterwards.

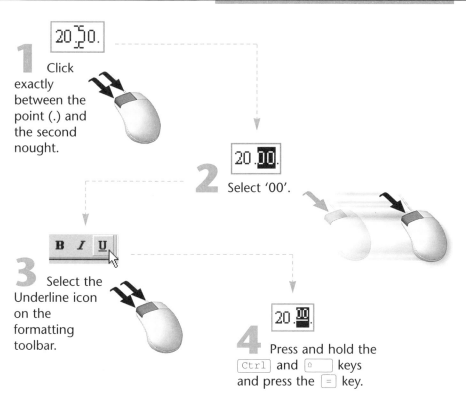

1 Click exactly between the point (.) and the second nought.

2 Select '00'.

3 Select the Underline icon on the formatting toolbar.

4 Press and hold the [Ctrl] and [⇧] keys and press the [=] key.

Scrolling through documents

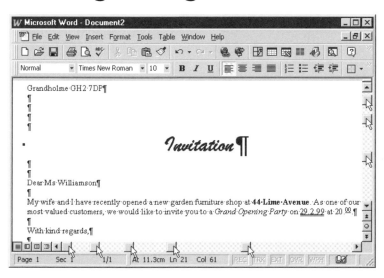

To look through
(scroll) a document
more quickly, use the
scroll bars on the right
of the screen.

The letter is finished. In Word, you always see only a screen section. As a rule, you cannot see the whole document at once. Use the cursor keys to see the top, bottom, left or right sections of your letter. The scroll bars on the right and bottom edges of the screen make it quicker to scan your document. Simply click on the small grey box inside the bar and, with the left mouse button pressed down, move it up or down (vertical scroll bar) or left or right (horizontal scroll bar), until the screen section you want appears.

If you want to look through the text line by line, click on one of the small triangles in the scroll bar.

The two 'double-arrow' buttons on the bottom edge of the vertical scroll bar provide another way of scrolling. These enable you to look through your document page by page.

1 Position the mouse pointer on the small grey box in the scroll bar (known as the scroll box), ...

2 ... and drag it right up to the top.

Saving a letter

We want to store the letter we have written so that we can work on it again later and keep it on our files. As in 'real life', we want to store the document away in a folder. Otherwise your documents would be irretrievably lost – as though you had put them in a shredder.

To save documents, select the File/Save As menu option. Another, quicker way is to click on the Save icon, shown here in the margin, on the standard toolbar. The third way is to use the File/Close menu option. You will then be asked if you wish to save the changes you have made.

Whatever you select, you always get into the Save As dialog box. In the Save in box, enter

where (that is, in which folder) you want to file the letter. Enter the name you want to call the letter in the box alongside File name.

Word makes its own suggestion for a file name, automatically using the beginning of the first line of text. Do not accept the suggestion, but type another name, such as 'Invitation', for example. If the suggested name is selected in blue, you can type the name without further ado. Word will automatically type over the Save suggestion in the blue selection. If you have already clicked in another input box, you must then manually delete the file name suggested by Word. When you click the Save button, the document is immediately stored under the name 'Invitation'.

If you want to edit the letter again later, click on the Save icon on the standard toolbar, and Word will again save the document including the changes. The Save As dialog box will no longer be displayed in this case.

63

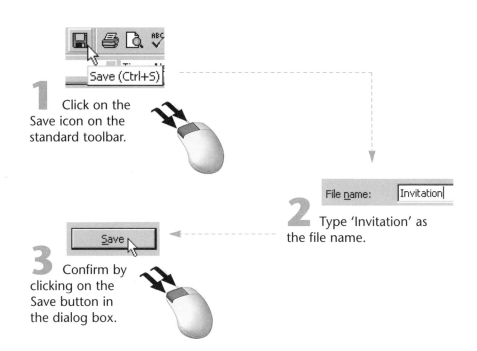

1 Click on the Save icon on the standard toolbar.

2 Type 'Invitation' as the file name.

File name: Invitation

3 Confirm by clicking on the Save button in the dialog box.

Once the document has been saved, the name which you have just given it will be displayed in the title bar. From now on, your first document is filed under the name 'Invitation'.

W Microsoft Word - Invitation

Print Preview

Naturally, we want to print our letter. But first let's check it using Print Preview. It is a preview of what will subsequently be printed and shows the document exactly as it will be printed out.

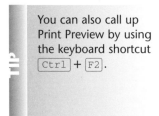

TIP
You can also call up Print Preview by using the keyboard shortcut Ctrl + F2.

Whereas a trial print run would be an unnecessary waste of paper, we can usually spot mistakes immediately using Print Preview. In other words, we always check the document first in the Print Preview, in order to make any corrections.

You cannot, however, enter or change anything while you are in Print Preview. You must first return to your document. Use the Close button to do this.

 You will see a magnifying glass in Print Preview. Clicking either of the mouse buttons will enlarge the view, another click will reduce it again.

1 Activate Print Preview on the standard toolbar.

2 You will see how the letter is laid out.

65

Invitation

Dear Ms Williamson

My wife and I have recently opened a new garden furniture shop at **44 Lime Avenue**. As one of our most valued customers, we would like to invite you to a *Grand Opening Party* on 29.2.99 at 20.⁰⁰.

With kind regards,

3 Enlarge the view by clicking the mouse in the text.

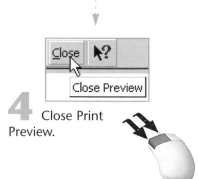

Instead of clicking on the Close button, you can also press the Esc button.

4 Close Print Preview.

Printing

Of course it's not the computer we want to send (that would cost far too much in postage!), but the document. Therefore it has to be printed out. To do this, click on the Print icon on the standard toolbar. It is easy to recognize as it has a little picture of a printer. One copy of the document will be printed each time you click on the icon.

If you select the File/Print menu option, you can specify further instructions regarding printing. Here you can state how many copies you want in each print job. An animated printer symbol displayed in the status bar will show you that Word is now printing your letter.

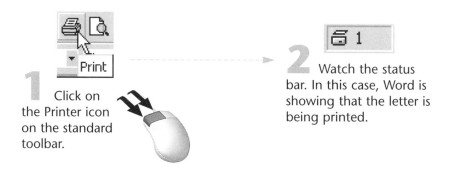

1 Click on the Printer icon on the standard toolbar.

2 Watch the status bar. In this case, Word is showing that the letter is being printed.

The Word Trainer

Exercise 1

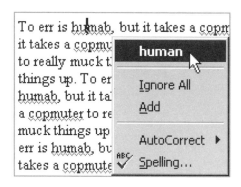

Are the following statements (t)rue or (f)alse:

◯ If you accept the word 'human', you will correct all words which are spelled incorrectly.

◯ If you select Add, the mistake will be ignored in all future documents.

◯ If you select Ignore All, the mistake will be ignored in all future documents.

Exercise 2

Create a new document (a new letter).

Exercise 3

Type the text below with the deliberate mistakes. You can also add your own mistakes. Correct the words which have been spelled incorrectly. You will find that Word is not perfect either, i.e. it does not know all the words.

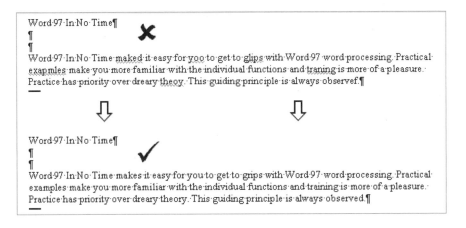

Exercise 4

Take the text from Exercise 3 and format it as follows:

1. Format the heading 'Word 97 In No Time' in Arial font, at size 16.

2. Centre the heading.

3. Format 'Word 97' in italics.

4. Put the word 'practice' in bold and underline it.

Word 97 In No Time

Word 97 In No Time makes it easy for you to get to grips with Word 97 word processing. Practical examples make you more familiar with the individual functions and training is more of a pleasure. **Practice** has priority over dreary theory. This guiding principle is always observed.

Exercise 5

Close Word. The next chapter deals with opening documents.

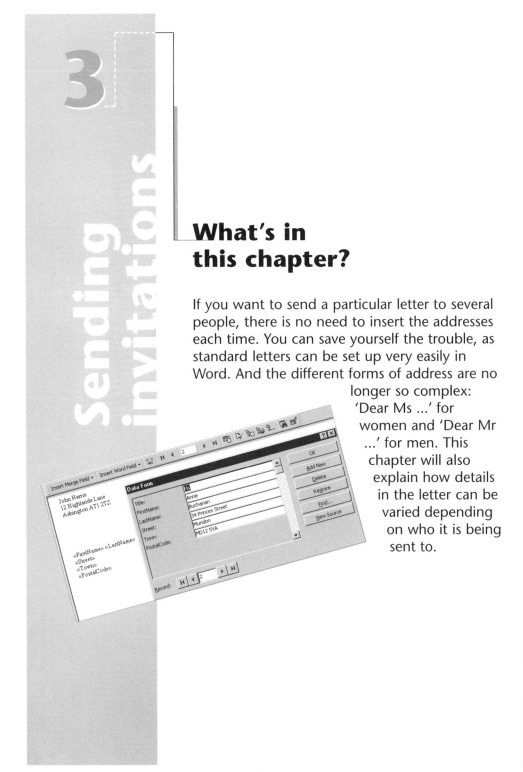

3

Sending invitations

What's in this chapter?

If you want to send a particular letter to several people, there is no need to insert the addresses each time. You can save yourself the trouble, as standard letters can be set up very easily in Word. And the different forms of address are no longer so complex: 'Dear Ms ...' for women and 'Dear Mr ...' for men. This chapter will also explain how details in the letter can be varied depending on who it is being sent to.

You already know:

You are going to learn:

Opening a document

For this section we need the 'Invitation' letter from the second chapter. If you haven't done it, you only have to type in the text and then you can start this section straight away.

For a saved document to appear on the screen again, it must be called up, or opened. As so often with Word, there are two ways of doing this: either select the File/Open menu option or click on the Open icon on the standard toolbar.

In the Look in box, enter where (i.e. in which folder) your letter has been filed. Then double-click on the File Name, and the document – listed here as Invitation – will be opened and displayed. You can also open the file by just double-clicking its icon in the Open dialog box.  Invitation

The Preview option is of interest here. It will always let you 'look inside' a document, without first having to open it. To do this, simply activate the Preview icon in the Open dialog box. Use the scroll bar to scroll through all of your document.

Deleting documents

You can also delete files in the Open dialog box. These will then be 'thrown' into the Windows 95 waste-paper basket. Just click on the document and press the Delete key. You can delete a document only if it is not open at that particular moment.

The last four ...

You will find a quick way of opening a document in the File menu. The names of the last documents to be saved are listed

right at the bottom. It is here that you will find our invitation – if you have saved the letter. The last four documents to be saved are shown. So if, after saving the letter, you were to save four other files, our invitation would no longer be included in the list.

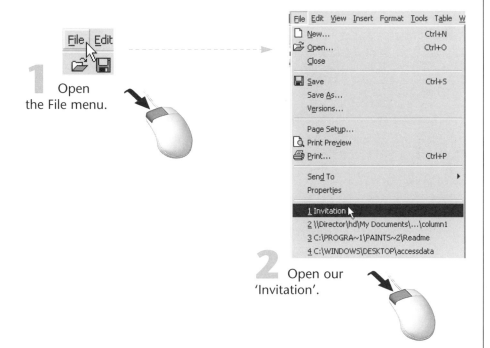

1 Open the File menu.

2 Open our 'Invitation'.

... will now become nine

But you can, however, also extend the list to a maximum of nine. To do this, select the

Tools/Options menu option. Switch to the General tab and increase the number of list entries. From now on the names of the last nine documents to be edited will be displayed in the File menu.

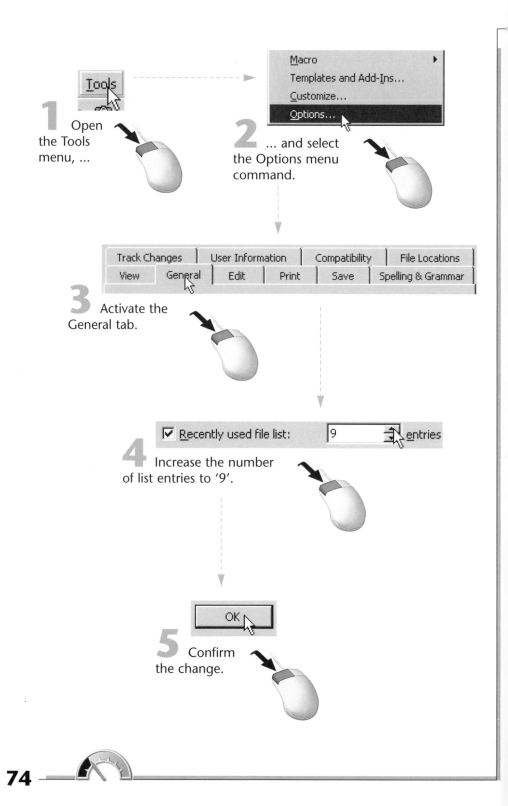

Macro ▶
Templates and Add-Ins...
Customize...
Options...

1 Open the Tools menu, ...

2 ... and select the Options menu command.

| Track Changes | User Information | Compatibility | File Locations |
| View | General | Edit | Print | Save | Spelling & Grammar |

3 Activate the General tab.

☑ Recently used file list: 9   entries

4 Increase the number of list entries to '9'.

OK

5 Confirm the change.

74

Standard letters

With Word, invitations can be sent to several people at the same time. How do you do this? You do not have to prepare a new letter each time, but instead you use the Mail Merge function. This function means that the addresses and titles do not have to be inserted each time.

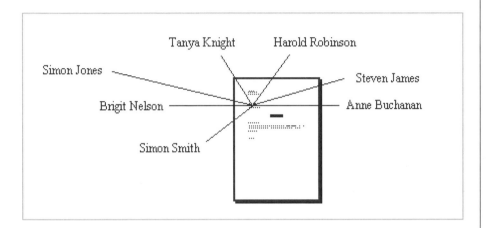

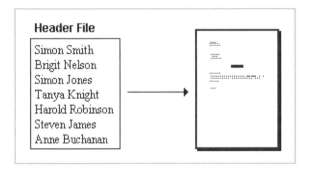

You simply enter the recipients' details (name, street, town etc.) in a separate file – called the header file – and merge these with the main document.

Deleting lines

The 'Invitation' document is displayed on the screen. As the invitation is to be sent to several people, we must first delete the original recipient's address.

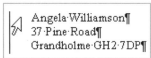

1 Position the mouse in front of the lines which are to be deleted.

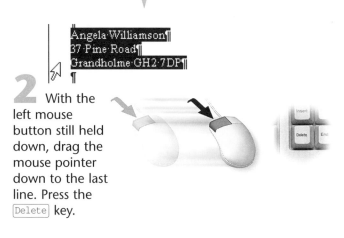

2 With the left mouse button still held down, drag the mouse pointer down to the last line. Press the `Delete` key.

Setting up the standard letter

And now we're ready to start! The first thing to do is to tell Word that you want to set up a standard letter. To do this, open the Tools menu and select the Mail Merge command.

This gets you into the Mail Merge Helper. As you want to set up standard letters, which Word calls Form Letters, you must click on the Create button under 1 Main document and select Form letters.

Now you can choose whether you want to use the active window or create a new main document. An Active Window means that you are referring to whatever document is open on the screen at that time.

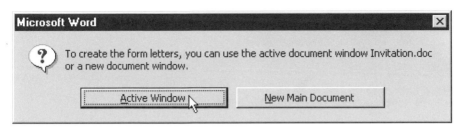

If you choose the New Main Document command you will start a new document. As the 'Invitation' document is already displayed on the screen, click on the Active Window button.

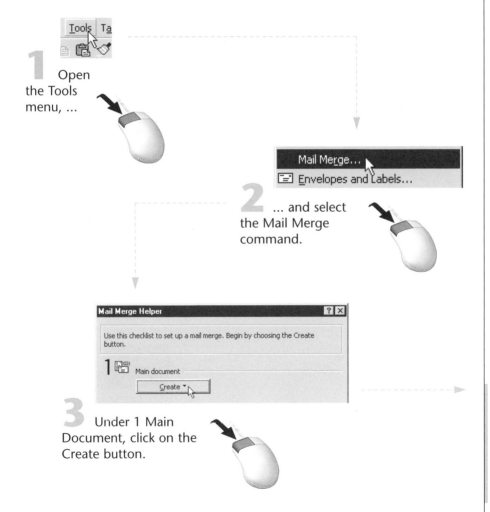

1 Open the Tools menu, ...

2 ... and select the Mail Merge command.

3 Under 1 Main Document, click on the Create button.

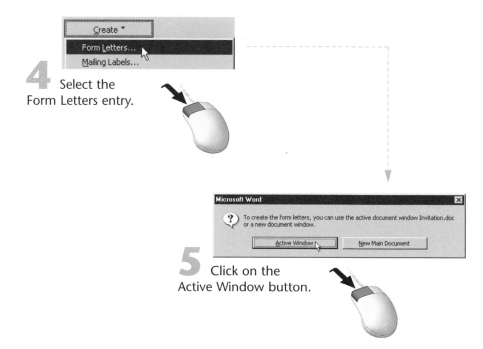

4 Select the Form Letters entry.

5 Click on the Active Window button.

The data source

You'll be returned to the Mail Merge Helper again. All that remains for you to do now is to enter the addresses for your invitations, in other words set up the data source. To do this, click on the Get Data button under 2 Data Source and select the Create Data Source entry.

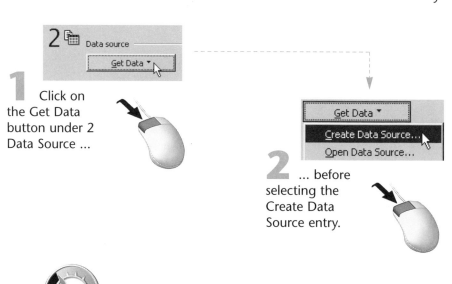

1 Click on the Get Data button under 2 Data Source ...

2 ... before selecting the Create Data Source entry.

Field Names

Some prior settings now have to be made for the standard letter you are going to send. You have to consider which fields you need in the letter, as these will be required at a future point. In the text, you will later be inserting the spaces for the title (form of address), name, street etc. These are called 'Field Names'.

Which fields do we need for our letter?

General	Example
Form of address	Mr
First Name Last Name	Steven Glover
Street	27 Wellington Road
Town and Postcode	Lordstown L94 7ZZ

Deleting field names

Word usually gives too many field names. For our standard letter, you can delete entries like 'JobTitle' or 'Address2'. To do this, first click on the relevant entry in the list under Field names in header row and then select the Delete Field Name button.

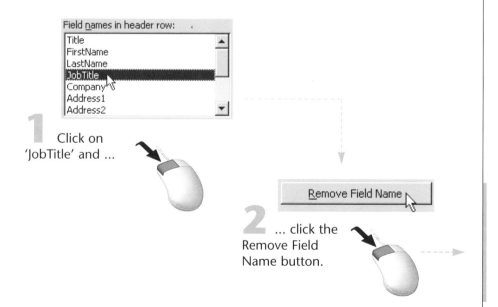

Field names in header row:

Title
FirstName
LastName
JobTitle
Company
Address1
Address2

1 Click on 'JobTitle' and ...

Remove Field Name

2 ... click the Remove Field Name button.

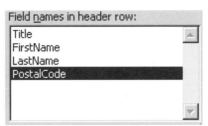

3 Repeat the first two steps and delete the following field names: Company, Address1, Address2, City, State, Country, HomePhone, and WorkPhone. The only field names left should be the ones shown above.

Inserting field names

You can enter new field names by using the Add Field Name button. Just type the new field name – in our example the 'Street' entry – and then click on the Add Field Name button.

Field name:

| Street|

1 Type 'Street' for the new field name.

Add Field Name ▶▶

2 Click on the Add Field Name button, and follow the same steps to add a 'Town' entry.

Sorting field names

The order of the entries (title, first name, last name, street, postcode, town) should correspond with the layout of the letter. This simplifies matters considerably later on. You can rearrange your list by using the Move arrow buttons.

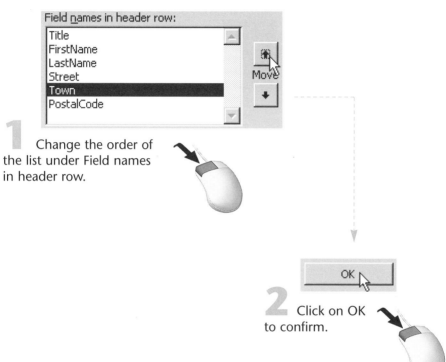

1 Change the order of the list under Field names in header row.

2 Click on OK to confirm.

Saving the data source

Use what are known as 'talking' names (such as Clients, Suppliers, Relations), so that later you will know which information is in which file. We are giving our example the name 'Addresses'.

Even though you are going to use it straight away, save your address file (i.e. all addresses) now, so that you can use it again for other mailshots.

81

Word tells you in a dialog box that the data source – i.e. our address file – still has to be compiled. No details have yet been given. Therefore click on the Edit Data Source button.

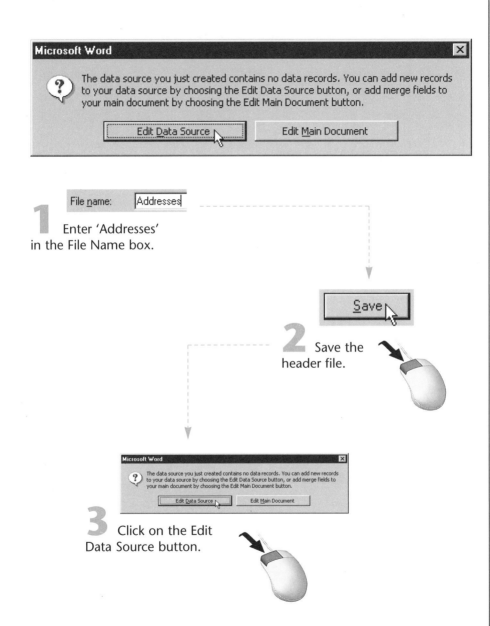

1 Enter 'Addresses' in the File Name box.

2 Save the header file.

3 Click on the Edit Data Source button.

Editing the data source

Enter your information for the fields in the Data Form Dialog.

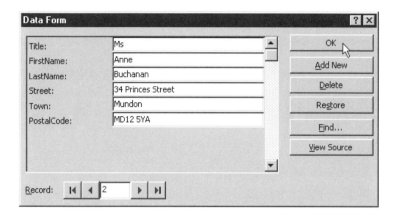

In this case, a Record comprises the details for a particular person, such as First Name, Last Name, Town, etc.

When you have completed your first entries (the first record), click on the Add New button. Then enter your second record. When you have entered all the addresses, exit the Data Form Dialog by clicking on the OK button.

To simplify the exercise, we are going to use only two addresses. That will be more than enough to explain the Mail Merge function. We shall, of course, be using a male and a female recipient.

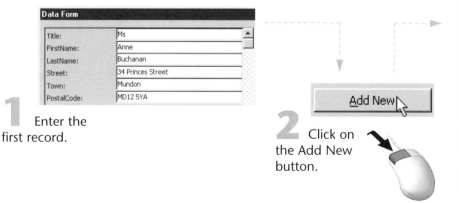

1 Enter the first record.

2 Click on the Add New button.

83

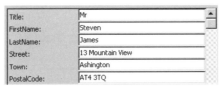

3 Enter the second record.

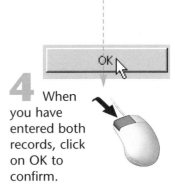

4 When you have entered both records, click on OK to confirm.

Adding Field Names

When you have exited the Data Form Dialog by clicking OK, you return to your document, in this case to our 'Invitation'. A new Toolbar with various mail merge functions is displayed on the screen.

How do you get back to the Data Form Dialog?

You can return to the Mail Merge Helper by clicking the Mail Merge Helper button in the Mail Merge toolbar.

Mail Merge Helper

When you have pressed the Edit button under 2 Data source, click on the Header File – i.e. the Address File – to return you to the Data Form Dialog, to add new records or make corrections, for example.

Now back to the 'Invitation' main document. You still have to enter the fields and where they should appear. Position the cursor in your document at exactly the point where the first field (in our case 'Title') should be inserted. Click the Insert Merge Field button in the Mail Merge toolbar. Now select the first field (in our case 'Title') from the list.

Enter the other mail merge fields (First Name, Last Name, Street, Town and Postal Code) in the correct order for the recipient field.

«Title» «FirstName» «LastName»¶
«Street»¶
«Town» «PostalCode»¶

If you stick to the arrangement of blank lines in the learning steps, your letter will fit into an envelope with a window, and, if correctly folded, the recipient field will appear in the correct position.

John·Harris¶
12·Highlands·Lane¶
Ashington·AT1·2TZ¶
¶
¶
¶
¶
¶
▮¶

1 Position the cursor exactly five lines under the Sender.

Insert Merge Field

2 Click on the Insert Merge Field button on the Mail Merge toolbar.

85

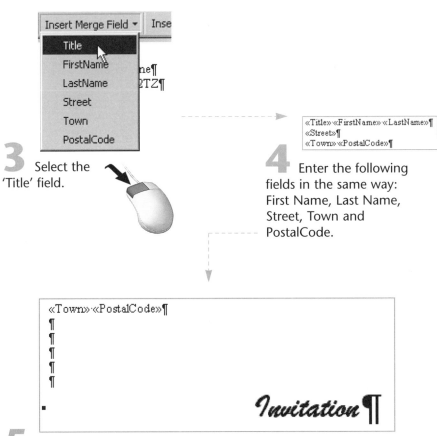

3 Select the 'Title' field.

4 Enter the following fields in the same way: First Name, Last Name, Street, Town and PostalCode.

5 There should be five blank lines between the recipient field and the subject matter of the letter.

Field functions – active or not

Whether or not your fields actually appear in the document depends on whether the Field Codes option in the View dialog box under the Tools/

Options/View menu is active. If it is switched on, the 'Title' field will be shown as above. If, on the other hand, the option is deactivated, it will look as shown below. It doesn't matter which appearance you opt for, as this does not affect the Mail Merge process.

¶
{MERGEFIELD·Title·}{MERGEFIELD·FirstName·}{MERGEFIELD·LastName·}¶
{MERGEFIELD·Street·}¶
{MERGEFIELD·Town·}{MERGEFIELD·PostalCode·}¶   ☑ Field codes

Personal text passages

It may be that you do not want everyone to receive exactly the same letter. In the case of our invitation, for instance, you might want to have a men-only night, with a ladies-only party on the next night. In that case, you might want to invite the male recipients on 28.2.99, and invite the women the following evening, 29.2.99. What do these two dates have in common? 2.99 occurs in both. Returning once again to our 'Invitation', we remove everything which is superfluous.

You are now going to add a condition. To do this, click on the Insert Word Field button on the mail merge bar.

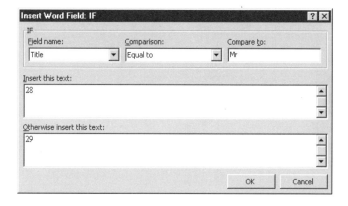

The computer knows only two possibilities: Yes or No. We can make good use of this.

If it is not a man, it can only be a woman. Is there a criterion by which Word can tell whether the recipient is a man or a woman? Yes, it is the Title field in the address file. This field is laid out separately, remember. If the recipient is a man, then 'Mr' is written here, if it is a woman, then 'Ms' is used instead. If the title field contains the word 'Mr', then Word should insert the date 28.2.99. If the title is not 'Mr', then 29.2.99 should be entered instead.

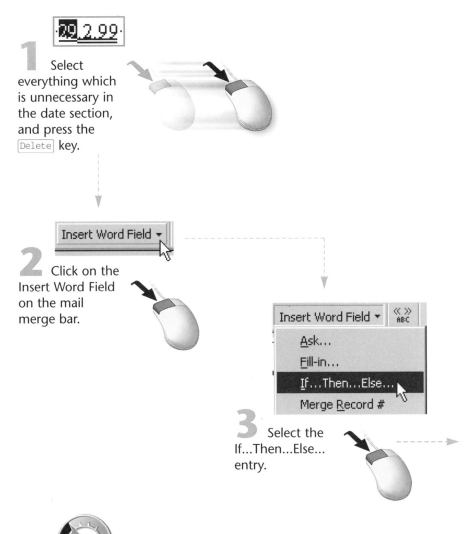

1 Select everything which is unnecessary in the date section, and press the `Delete` key.

2 Click on the Insert Word Field on the mail merge bar.

Insert Word Field ▾   《 》 ABC

Ask...
Fill-in...
If...Then...Else...
Merge Record #

3 Select the If...Then...Else... entry.

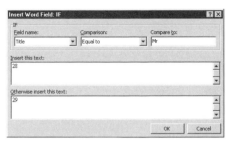

4 Enter the information
that follows, making sure
no full stops are entered.

5 Click on
OK to confirm.

The salutation

Our original document is addressed to Ms Williamson. Obviously,
this needs to be deleted and the title field added here instead. To do
this, insert a space after 'Dear' using the space bar and insert the
Title mail merge field.

In the salutation, the recipients will be called by their last names.

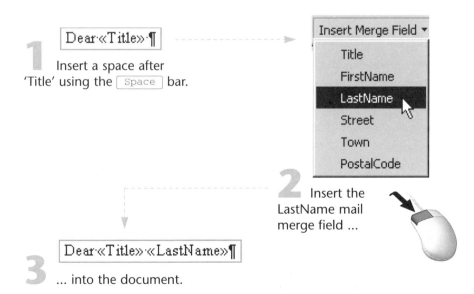

1 Insert a space after
'Title' using the Space bar.

2 Insert the
LastName mail
merge field ...

3 ... into the document.

89

More personal text passages

Just to complicate matters further, you decide men might respond better to being

most·valued·customers,

described as 'loyal' customers, rather than 'valued'. Again, we can use the If...Then...Else... function here. If the recipient is a man, the phrase will be 'most loyal customers', if not 'most valued customers'.

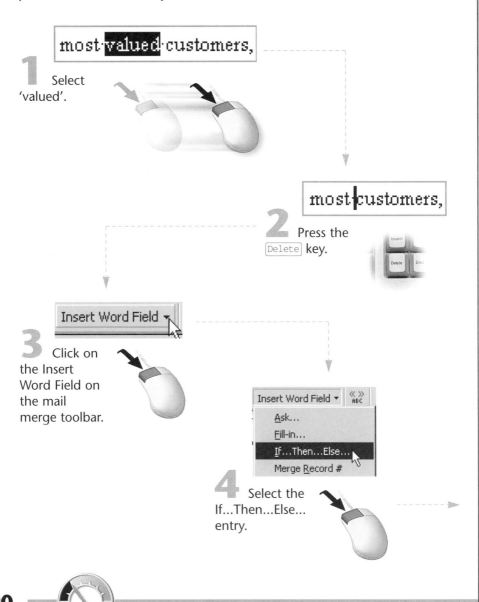

most valued customers,

1 Select 'valued'.

most customers,

2 Press the Delete key.

Insert Word Field ▾

3 Click on the Insert Word Field on the mail merge toolbar.

Insert Word Field ▾   « »
                       ABC

Ask...
Fill-in...
If...Then...Else...
Merge Record #

4 Select the If...Then...Else... entry.

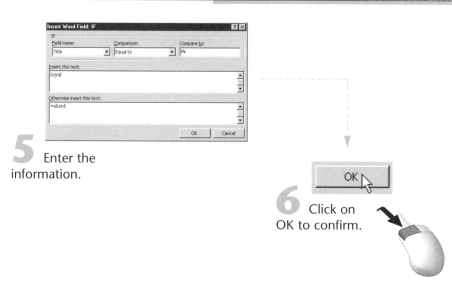

5 Enter the information.

6 Click on OK to confirm.

Merging the data source and the standard letter

By clicking on the View Merged Data button in the Mail Merge toolbar, you can check your standard letters on the screen before they are printed. Clicking the button a second time will return you to the main document.

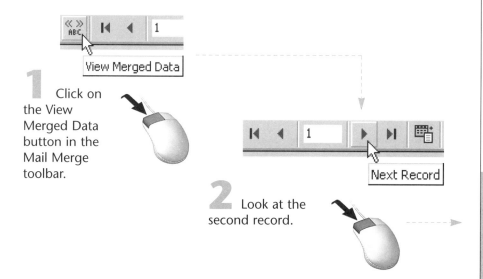

1 Click on the View Merged Data button in the Mail Merge toolbar.

View Merged Data

Next Record

2 Look at the second record.

3 If you do not find any errors, return to the main document.

4 Print the standard letters.

Closing Word and saving the document

When you exit Word, you are asked if you want to save the changes in the Invitation document and in the Address file. Click on Yes to confirm.

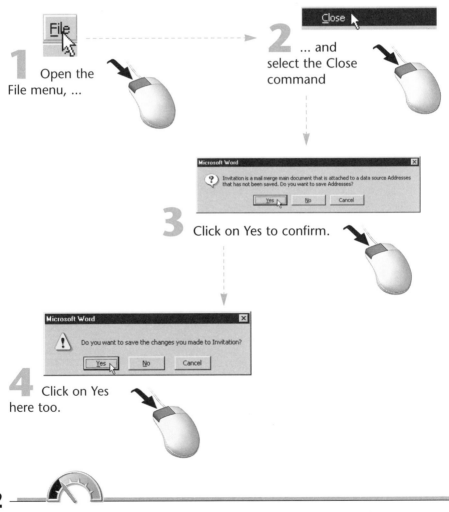

1 Open the File menu, ...

2 ... and select the Close command

Microsoft Word

Invitation is a mail merge main document that is attached to a data source Addresses that has not been saved. Do you want to save Addresses?

Yes   No   Cancel

3 Click on Yes to confirm.

Microsoft Word

Do you want to save the changes you made to Invitation?

Yes   No   Cancel

4 Click on Yes here too.

The Word Trainer

File the following data in an address file:

Title	First Name	Last Name	Street	Town	Post Code	Amount
Mr	Richard	Andrews	66 Hill View	Swansea	SA6 6CD	250
Mr	Gerald	Sorrell	15 Dean Street	Bristol	BR5 9EF	450
Ms	Beryl	Harrison	45 Maple Avenue	London	WC2 2GH	890
Mr	Louis	Davies	1 Longridge Road	Blackpool	BL2 4IJ	300
Mr	Christopher	Bates	7 Parkway	Watford	WD40 5KL	120
Ms	Karen	Henson	88 Coronation Drive	Ipswich	IP3 7MN	450

Now create the standard letter. For people owing £300 or more, this is a final reminder. Use If ... Then ... If not ... to solve this problem.

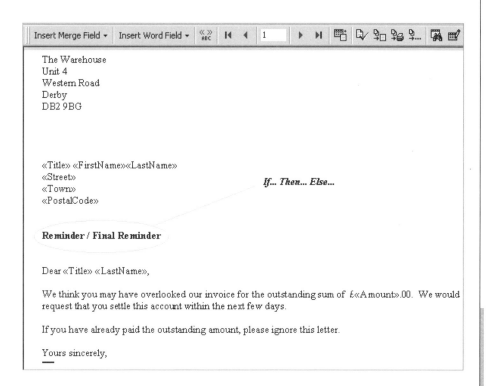

4

The list
of addresses

What's in
this chapter?

Are you always just jotting down your family's,
friends' and acquaintances' addresses,
telephone numbers and birthdays on little
scraps of paper? Not any more, you won't! In
this chapter, we are going to file a clearly laid
out list of addresses
and sort it into
alphabetical order, so
that you won't
'forget' important
dates, occasions
and appointments
ever again.

Last Name	First Name	Address List ✉	Birthday	☎ 081 696 4480
Black	Sylvia	45 Maple Avenue London WC2 2GH	02.01.58	0330 457729
Denton	Alice	88 Coronation Drive Ipswich IP3 7MN	22.12.53	0330 457729
Denton	John	88 Coronation Drive Ipswich IP3 7MN	07.07.54	061 880 9126
Summers	Graeme	282 Caledonia Way Edinburgh EB8 0JG	31.05.78	0296 422915
Summers	Rosemary	66 Hill View Swansea SA6 6CD	03.07.62	0145 238041
Thompson	Adam	15 Dean Street Bristol BR5 9EF	25.08.67	0145 238041
Thompson	Susan	15 Dean Street Bristol BR5 9EF	04.08.72	0502 537311
Thomson	Graham	1 Longridge Road Blackpool BL2 4LJ	03.01.71	

You already know:

You are going to learn:

95

Inserting a table

Formatting the heading

When formatting the first line, always first use the Return key to move to the next line. Otherwise the formats for the first line will be repeated each time the ⎯ key is used.

Before keying in our list of addresses, we must first write the heading. What could be better than 'Address List'?

We format the heading so that it 'catches the reader's eye', centre the line and change the font and font size.

Address List

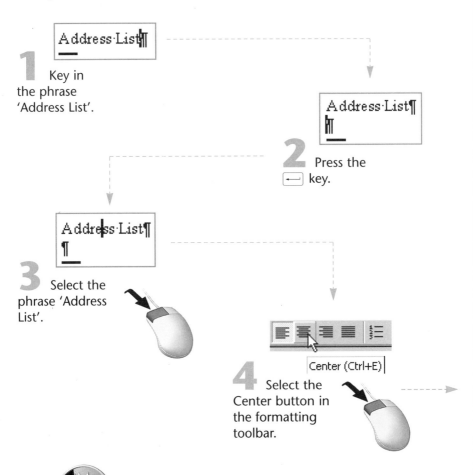

1 Key in the phrase 'Address List'.

2 Press the ⎯ key.

3 Select the phrase 'Address List'.

Center (Ctrl+E)

4 Select the Center button in the formatting toolbar.

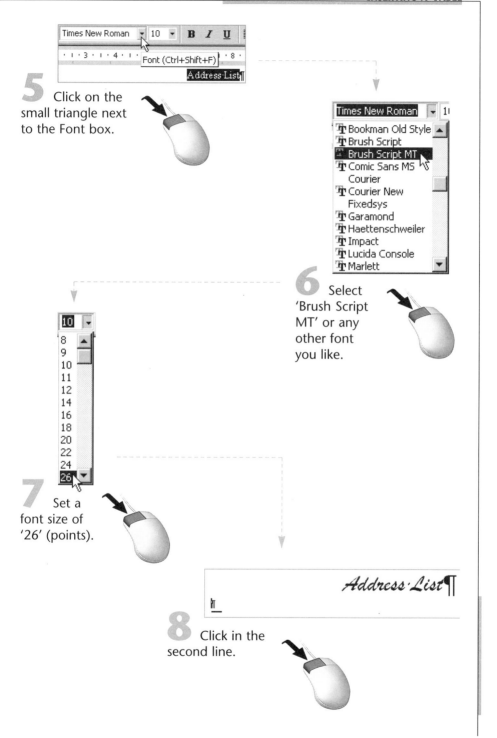

5 Click on the small triangle next to the Font box.

6 Select 'Brush Script MT' or any other font you like.

7 Set a font size of '26' (points).

8 Click in the second line.

Address·List¶

Creating a table

A table is made up of rows and columns.

The very fact that Word has its own Table menu shows how often tables are used.

To create a table, select the Table/Insert Table menu option and then enter the number of rows and columns. It is quicker if you use the Insert Table icon on the Standard toolbar.

If you click on the icon, a drop-down menu appears where you can specify the number of rows and columns the tables should have.

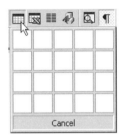

You do not need to press any mouse buttons, but just move the mouse pointer until the numbers of rows and columns you want are shown below. Then click the left mouse button to confirm. The outlines of the table will then appear in the document. Two rows are enough to begin with for our example. We then define the columns for Last Name, First Name, Address and Telephone Number (four columns).

If you have made a mistake when creating your table, you can cancel the last command by clicking on the Undo icon.

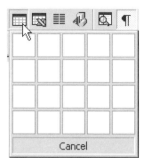

1 Click on the Insert Table icon on the standard toolbar.

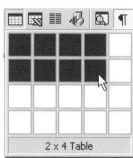

2 Specify two rows and four columns (2 x 4).

3 Click on the mouse to confirm.

The table header

We specify the table heading or table header in the first row.

Click on one cell and enter your text. In our example the cursor is still flashing in the top left cell. Key in 'Last Name' here. Press the ⬌ key to move into the next cell.

| Last Name¤ | ¤ |
| ¤ | ¤ |

Type 'First Name' in the second column header. Something special is going to happen with the last two columns. More on that later!

You move from cell to cell using the ⬌ key. But you can also go from one cell to another by clicking on the cell you want to go to with the mouse. Or you can use the arrow keys to move about in tables ⬆, ⬇, ⬅, ➡.

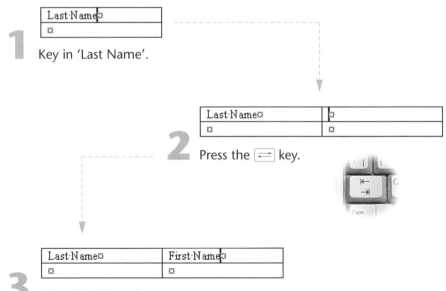

1 Key in 'Last Name'.

| Last Name¤ | |
| ¤ | |

2 Press the ⬌ key.

| Last Name¤ | ¤ |
| ¤ | ¤ |

3 Enter 'First Name'.

| Last Name¤ | First Name¤ |
| ¤ | ¤ |

So that Word recognises that the first row in our table represents the table's headings, we specify this by using the Table/Headings menu option. This is very important if the document is to be clearly laid out later on. If you have a lot of friends, relations and acquaintances, the table will spread over one page. By using the Headings command, the heading will appear on each new page.

✓ Headings

The tick tells you that the heading is activated.

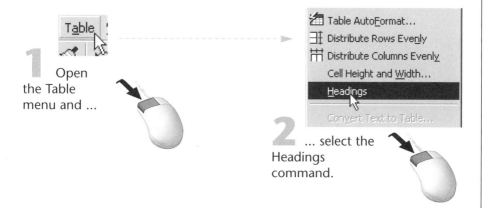

1 Open the Table menu and ...

🖀 Table Auto**F**ormat...
⊟ Distribute Rows Eve**n**ly
▦ Distribute Columns Evenl**y**
  Cell Height and **W**idth...
  Headings
  Con**v**ert Text to Table...

2 ... select the Headings command.

Inserting symbols

To make our list of addresses more varied, we are going to add symbols. Word offers a wide range of symbols. Use the menu option Insert/Symbol. You will see a range of fonts. The most suitable in this case is definitely Wingdings.

Wingdings is a font which contains arrows and symbols.

Here you will find symbols for everyday use. They look rather small. But if you click the left mouse button on one of the symbols it will be shown magnified. You can also move about using the arrow keys ⬆, ⬇, ⬅, ➡.

Any symbol you select will look larger. If you want to use a particular symbol, insert it by double-clicking the left mouse button or using the Insert button. You must first position the cursor in your document where the symbol is to be inserted.

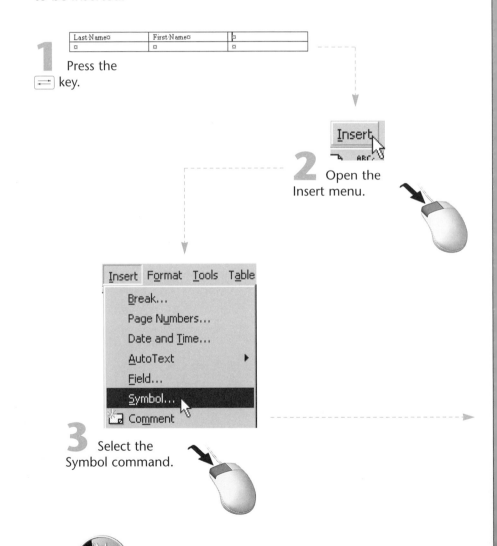

1 Press the ⇄ key.

| Last·Name¤ | First·Name¤ | ¤ |
| ¤ | ¤ | ¤ |

2 Open the Insert menu.

Insert

3 Select the Symbol command.

Insert Format Tools Table

Break...
Page Numbers...
Date and Time...
AutoText ▶
Field...
Symbol...
Comment

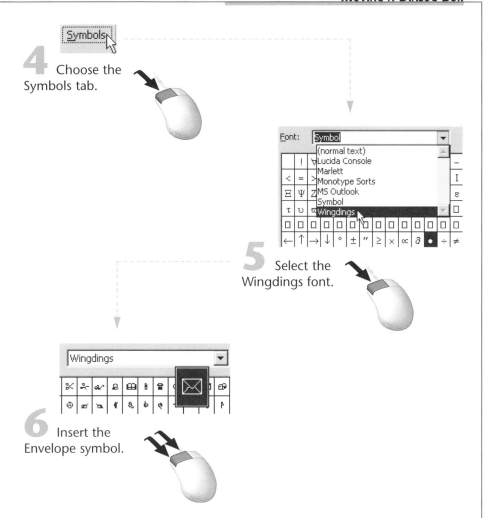

4 Choose the Symbols tab.

5 Select the Wingdings font.

6 Insert the Envelope symbol.

Moving a dialog box

Where the dialog box is positioned on your screen at present makes it difficult to see our table, so we are going to move it to get a better view of the entries made. To do this, click on the Title bar of the dialog box and hold the left mouse button down.

103

Drag the window down until you can see the table entries better. When moving the box, you will see a broken line.

1 Click on the title bar of the dialog box and, holding the left mouse key down, ...

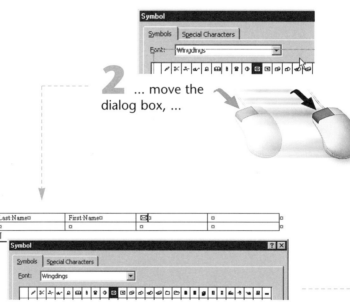

2 ... move the dialog box, ...

3 ... until you get a better view of the table.

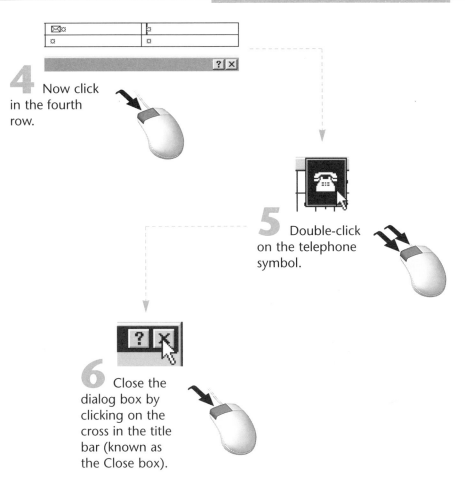

4 Now click in the fourth row.

5 Double-click on the telephone symbol.

6 Close the dialog box by clicking on the cross in the title bar (known as the Close box).

Entering the text into the table

And now we can get on to actually entering the text into the table. You enter your data cell by cell using the ⊡ key. If, however, you want to file more addresses, you will need more rows. When you are in the last cell, press the ⊡ key again, and Word will add a new table row.

Incidentally, some of the proper names in our address list won't be in Word's dictionary, so Word considers them to be wrong and

105

underlines them with the 'red wavy line'. You can leave it like that, as it will not make any difference to the document when it is printed. Alternatively – if it irritates you – you can cancel the function by selecting the Ignore All command for each individual word. You can also totally switch off the spell checker by selecting the Spelling and Grammar tab using the Tools/Options command.

Last·Name¤	First·Name¤	✉¤	☎¤
Summers¤	Rosemary¤	66·Hill·View¶ Swansea·SA6·6CD¤	0296·422915¤
Thompson¤	Susan¤	15·Dean·Street¶ Bristol·BR5·9EF¤	0145·238041¤
Black¤	Sylvia¤	45·Maple·Avenue¶ London·WC2·2GH¤	081·696·4480¤
Thomson¤	Graham¤	1·Longridge·Road¶ Blackpool·B	0502·537311¤
Thompson¤	Adam¤	15·Dean·Str Bristol·BR5·	
Denton¤	John¤	88·Coronati Ipswich·IP3·	
Summers¤	Graeme¤	282·Caledo Edinburgh·E	

(no spelling suggestions)
Ignore All
Add
Spelling…

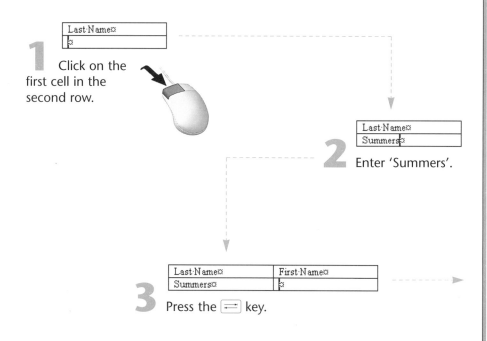

Last·Name¤

1 Click on the first cell in the second row.

Last·Name¤
Summers¤

2 Enter 'Summers'.

Last·Name¤	First·Name¤
Summers¤	

3 Press the ⏎ key.

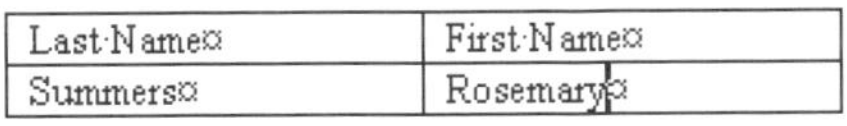

Last·Name¤	First·Name¤
Summers¤	Rosemary¤

4 Type 'Rosemary'.

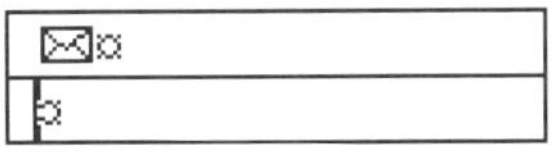

⊠¤

¤

5 Press the ⇄ key again.

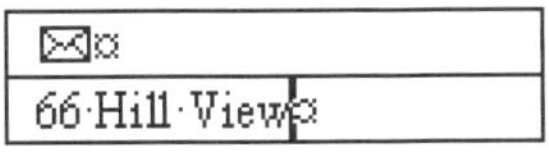

⊠¤

66·Hill·View¤

6 Then enter '66 Hill View'.

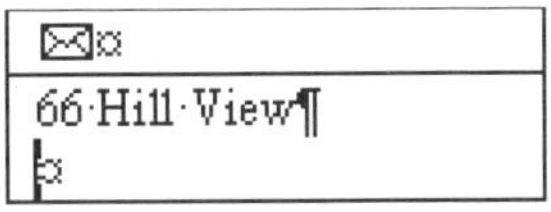

⊠¤

66·Hill·View¶
¤

7 Press the ← key.

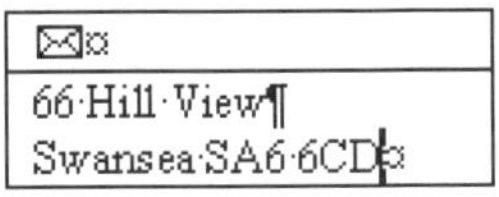

⊠¤

66·Hill·View¶
Swansea·SA6·6CD¤

8 Type 'Swansea SA6 6CD'.

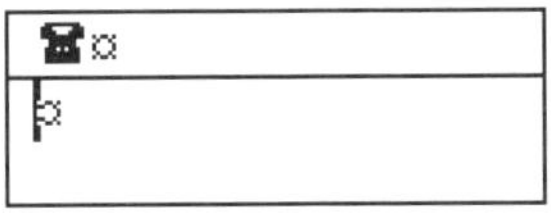

☎¤

¤

9 Press the ⇄ key.

107

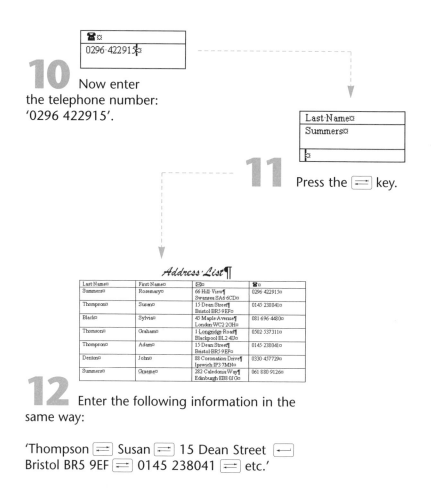

10 Now enter the telephone number: '0296 422915'.

11 Press the ⇌ key.

Address List¶

Last Name¤	First Name¤	✉¤	☎¤
Summers¤	Rosemary¤	66 Hill View¶ Swansea SA6 6CD¤	0296 422915¤
Thompson¤	Susan¤	15 Dean Street¶ Bristol BR5 9EF¤	0145 238041¤
Black¤	Sylvia¤	45 Maple Avenue¶ London WC2 2GH¤	081 696 4480¤
Thomson¤	Graham¤	1 Longridge Road¶ Blackpool BL2 4JJ¤	0502 537311¤
Thompson¤	Adam¤	15 Dean Street¶ Bristol BR5 9EF¤	0145 238041¤
Denton¤	John¤	88 Coronation Drive¶ Ipswich IP3 7MN¤	0330 457729¤
Summers¤	Graeme¤	282 Caledonia Way¶ Edinburgh EB8 0JO¤	061 880 9126¤

12 Enter the following information in the same way:

'Thompson ⇌ Susan ⇌ 15 Dean Street ←
Bristol BR5 9EF ⇌ 0145 238041 ⇌ etc.'

Selecting cells, rows and columns

Selecting cells

We want to format our table a little bit more. We are now going to format the 'Last Name' and 'First Name' column headings in the table header in bold. We do this by selecting both cells. Click on the first cell and, holding the mouse button down, drag to the next cell.

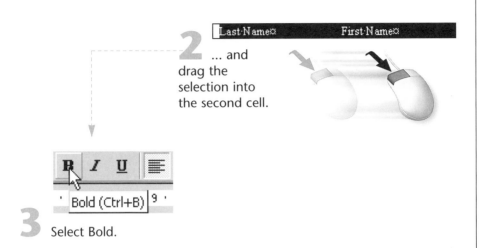

1 Click on the first cell, hold the mouse button down ...

2 ... and drag the selection into the second cell.

3 Select Bold.

Selecting columns

In our table, we are going to centre the contents of the third and fourth columns. First, select both columns. To do this, position the mouse pointer on the top line. The mouse pointer will change into a black downward-pointing arrow. This means that the whole column can now be selected by simply clicking on the left mouse button. Drag the mouse pointer into the next column to select it too. Now click on the Center icon in the formatting bar and the contents will be aligned immediately.

109

1 Select the third column.

2 Drag the selection into the fourth column.

Center (Ctrl+E)

3 Click on the Center icon on the formatting toolbar.

Selecting rows

We can enlarge the table header a little by selecting a different font size. To do this, we need to select a row.

When the mouse pointer is positioned to the left of a row, it changes the direction in which it points. Click the left mouse button, and the column is selected. If you want to select several rows, simply drag the selection up or down.

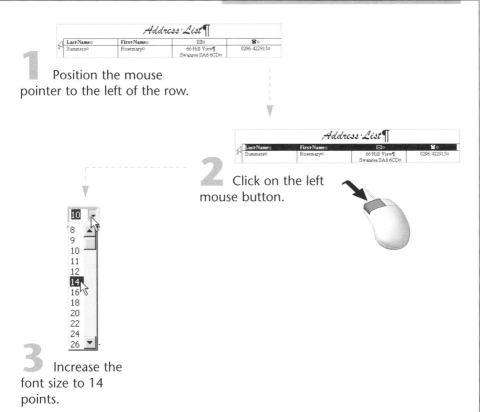

1 Position the mouse pointer to the left of the row.

2 Click on the left mouse button.

3 Increase the font size to 14 points.

Inserting rows and columns

Inserting rows

Mr 'Denton, John' is one of the entries in our example. He has now got married. Naturally, we want to include his wife in our list of addresses. The entry can go above or below 'Denton, John', because all we are doing at the moment is adding cells within a table.

The Insert Rows icon on the standard toolbar is important. It appears only when the cursor is inside a table. You will find the same function under the Table/Insert Rows menu option. You can delete rows from a table in the same way (Table/ Delete Rows).

111

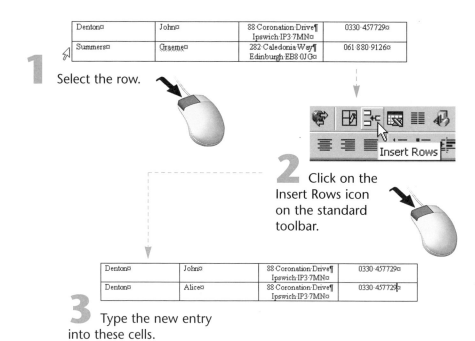

Select the row.

Click on the Insert Rows icon on the standard toolbar.

Type the new entry into these cells.

Inserting a column

We would also like to insert a 'Birthdays' column in our table, so that we do not forget to send people a card.

As soon as you select a column, the Insert Rows icon changes into Insert Columns.

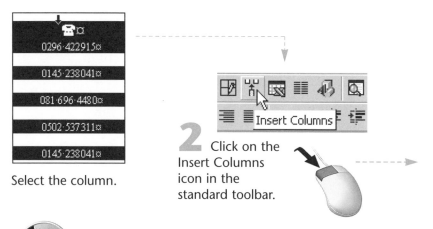

Select the column.

Click on the Insert Columns icon in the standard toolbar.

Birthday¤
03.07.62¤
04.08.72¤
02.01.58¤
03.01.71¤
25.08.67¤
07.07.54¤
22.12.53¤
31.05.78¤

3 Enter the details.

Changing the width of a column

Now that we have inserted the extra column, we can hardly see our list of addresses. You could set the Zoom function so that the table once again 'fits' on the screen. But this would make the writing so small that you would have to use a magnifying glass to see what was on your monitor.

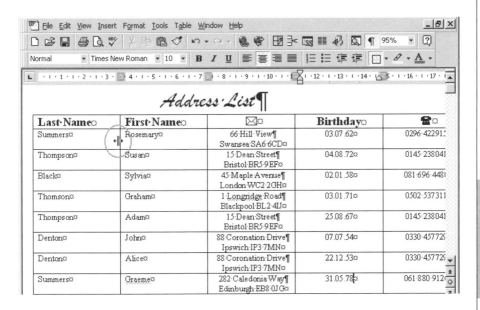

The 'Last Name' and 'First Name' columns take up so much space unnecessarily, that we would like to reduce them. If the mouse pointer is placed between two columns, it changes its appearance.

 Holding the mouse button down, drag the column line. If you press the right mouse button while moving the column, the exact column width will be displayed in the ruler.

 Alternatively, you can also change the width on the ruler.

For exceptionally large tables, you can select landscape format on the Paper Size tab, having used the File/Page Setup option.

Of course, you do not have to stick exactly to the centimetres shown in our example. All that matters is that you understand the principle.

Position the mouse pointer on the column line.

With the mouse button pressed down, drag the mouse pointer slightly to the left, ...

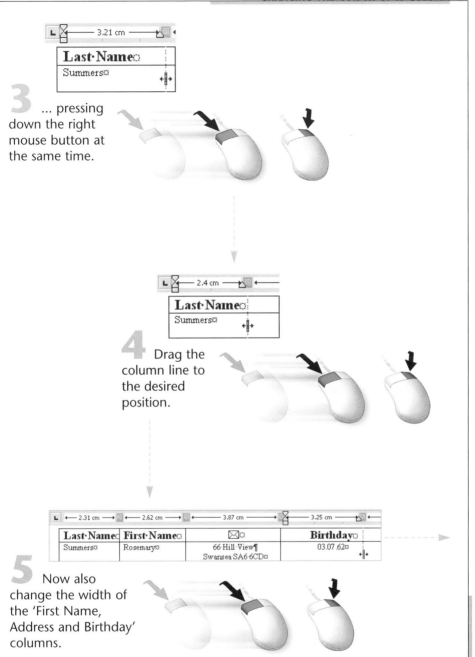

3 ... pressing down the right mouse button at the same time.

4 Drag the column line to the desired position.

5 Now also change the width of the 'First Name, Address and Birthday' columns.

115

Summers¤ | Graeme¤

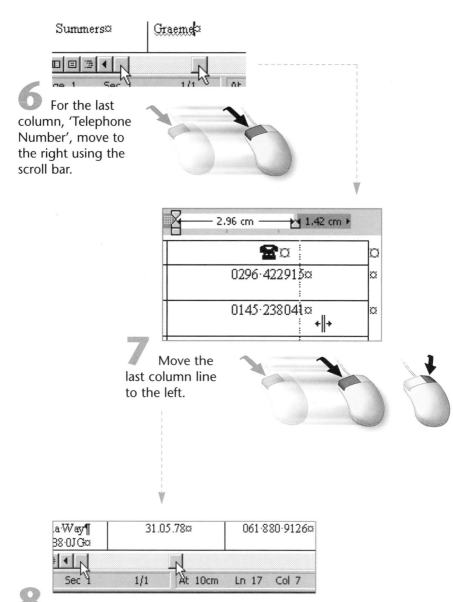

6 For the last column, 'Telephone Number', move to the right using the scroll bar.

2.96 cm — 1.42 cm ►

☎¤

0296·422915¤

0145·238041¤

7 Move the last column line to the left.

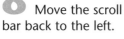

a·Way¶
38·0JG¤

31.05.78¤ | 061·880·9126¤

Sec 1 | 1/1 | At 10cm | Ln 17 | Col 7

8 Move the scroll bar back to the left.

In Word, you can also modify tables according to the length and height of the text. To do this, select the whole table (click on Select Table in the Table menu). Select the Cell Height and Width menu option, choose 'Auto' under Height of rows in the Row tab. Then select the Column tab and click the AutoFit button. The cells will now be just the size required for the text.

Sorting table entries

We have now nearly finished our list of addresses, but the individual names are rather higgledy-piggledy. It would be better to arrange them alphabetically.

Address·List¶

Last·Name¤	First·Name¤	⊠¤	Birthday¤	☎¤	¤
Summers¤	Rosemary¤	66·Hill·View¶ Swansea·SA6·6CD¤	03.07.62¤	0296·422915¤	¤
Thompson¤	Susan¤	15·Dean·Street¶ Bristol·BR5·9EF¤	04.08.72¤	0145·238041¤	¤
Black¤	Sylvia¤	45·Maple·Avenue¶ London·WC2·2GH¤	02.01.58¤	081·696·4480¤	¤
Thomson¤	Graham¤	1·Longridge·Road¶ Blackpool·BL2·4IJ¤	03.01.71¤	0502·537311¤	¤
Thompson¤	Adam¤	15·Dean·Street¶ Bristol·BR5·9EF¤	25.08.67¤	0145·238041¤	¤
Denton¤	John¤	88·Coronation·Drive¶ Ipswich·IP3·7MN¤	07.07.54¤	0330·457729¤	¤
Denton¤	Alice¤	88·Coronation·Drive¶ Ipswich·IP3·7MN¤	22.12.53¤	0330·457729¤	¤
Summers¤	Graeme¤	282·Caledonia·Way¶ Edinburgh·EB8·0JG¤	31.05.78¤	061·880·9126¤	¤

The example we are using presents a slight problem. We have entered people who have the same surnames. These are 'Thompson' and 'Summers'. We want to sort the entries as in a telephone directory, i.e., the last name will be listed first, followed by the first name

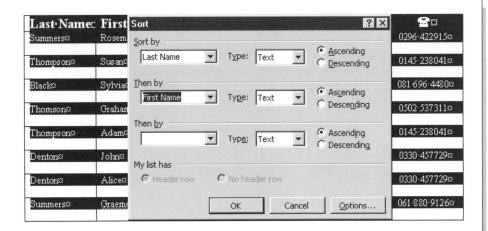

Select the Table/Sort menu option and specify the criteria using the sort keys. Word will automatically select the table in the background.

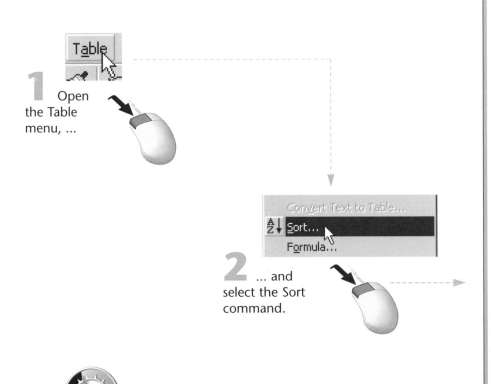

1 Open the Table menu, ...

2 ... and select the Sort command.

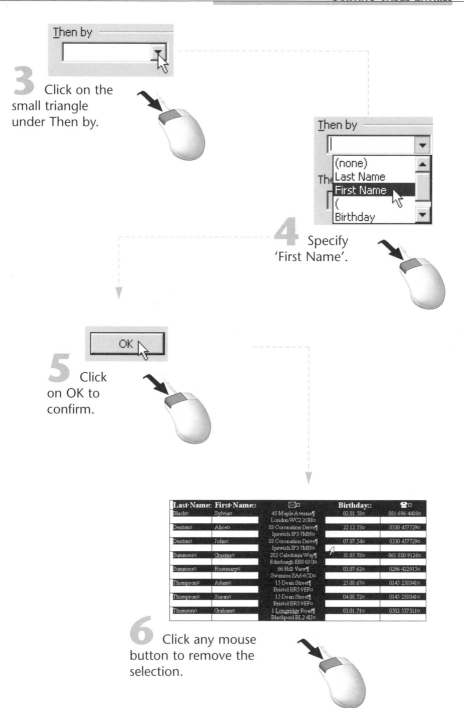

3 Click on the small triangle under Then by.

4 Specify 'First Name'.

5 Click on OK to confirm.

6 Click any mouse button to remove the selection.

The Tables Trainer

In this exercise, we are going to have a more detailed look at sorting tables. This time, we are not going to list text, but figures instead.

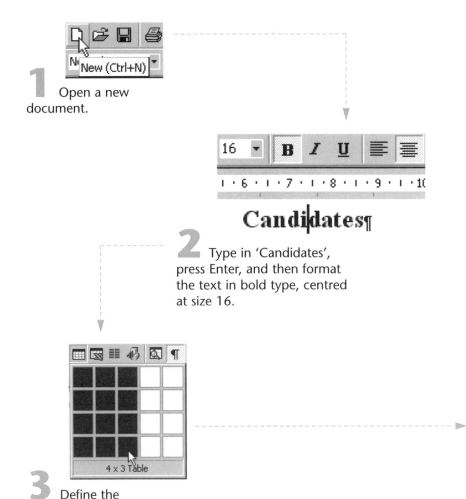

1 Open a new document.

2 Type in 'Candidates', press Enter, and then format the text in bold type, centred at size 16.

3 Define the table as shown.

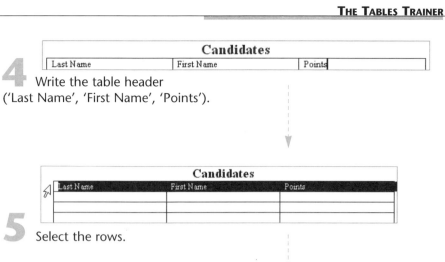

4 Write the table header
('Last Name', 'First Name', 'Points').

5 Select the rows.

6 Format the cell
contents in Bold.

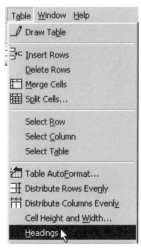

7 Select the Headings
command.

Candidates		
Last Name	First Name	Points
Collins	David	89
Burton	James	52
Wilson	Richard	92

8 Now type in the cell contents.

9 Open the Table menu ...

10 ... and select the Sort command.

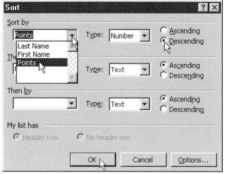

11 We want the person with the highest number of points to be shown in first place, so specify 'Points' under Sort by. As we want the marks to be sorted from 100 to 0, and not from 0 to 100, select the Descending option. Click OK to confirm.

Candidates		
Last Name	First Name	Points
Wilson	Richard	92
Collins	David	89
Burton	James	52

12 And this is what the result looks like: The winner with the highest number of points is at the top.

What's in this chapter?

You have been burgled and all your valuables have gone. What a terrible thought! And no one knows exactly what 'they' have taken. Piggy banks, hi-fi, the jewellery left to you by Grandma, Grandpa's old pocket watch? The best thing to do would be to make an inventory beforehand. That way, you won't have any trouble with the insurance company later and you will always know how much you should insure your valuables for. So get rid of all those receipts kept in shoe boxes. Simply file away the receipts or invoices for things and let Word help you draw up a list.

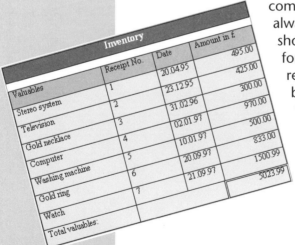

Inventory			
Valuables	Receipt No.	Date	Amount in £
Stereo system	1	20.04.95	495.00
Television	2	23.12.95	425.00
Gold necklace	3	31.02.96	300.00
Computer	4	02.01.97	970.00
Washing machine	5	10.01.97	500.00
Gold ring	6	20.09.97	833.00
Watch	7	21.09.97	1500.99
Total valuables:			5023.99

You already know:

You are going to learn:

The Draw Table function

You can design your own tables by using the Draw Table function. Use the Table/Draw Table menu option or click on the Tables and Borders

button. Whichever one you choose, another toolbar is opened on your screen. This will offer you a great many options, which we shall go into in more detail during this

chapter. However, you already know the function of the A to Z and Z to A buttons. We use them to sort tables, but only the first column. Further along in the toolbar, you will also find the Draw Table option.

If you click on the Draw Table icon, the mouse pointer will change to look like a pencil. To get it back to the ordinary mouse pointer, click again on the icon or press Esc.

You use the pencil to define the tables and also the individual cells to suit your requirements, as you can see from the slightly 'abstract' example shown here.

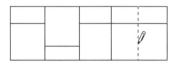

Click at the point where you want to start drawing and drag with mouse button pressed down. You can produce horizontal or vertical lines, but not diagonal lines.

If you draw a line wrong in the table by mistake, there is no need to re-design the whole table. Just click on the Undo icon, and Word will cancel the last command.

1 Click on the Tables and Borders icon on the standard toolbar.

2 Position the pencil to the left of your document, hold the left mouse button down, and ...

3 ... create the first row of the table.

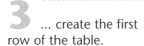

4 Re-position the pencil.

127

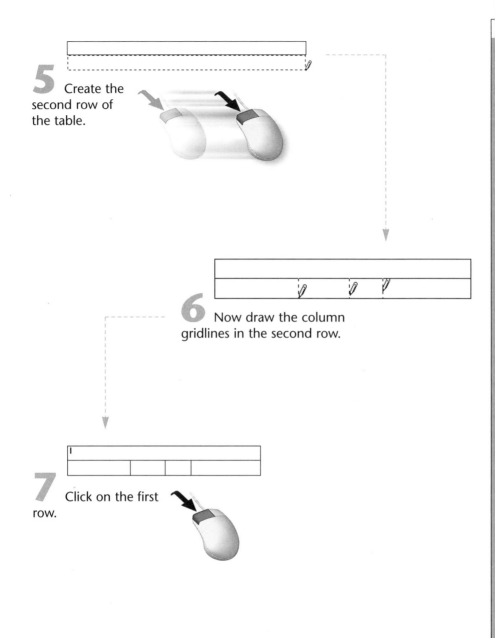

5 Create the
second row of
the table.

6 Now draw the column
gridlines in the second row.

7 Click on the first
row.

Adding colour

Inventory			
I			

What is adding colour on a computer all about? It is just the same as when you colour a white sheet of paper red. You change the colour of an area in a table in exactly the same way.

Click on the triangle by the Shading Colour icon and select a colour. You will return to the 'Norm' by selecting None.

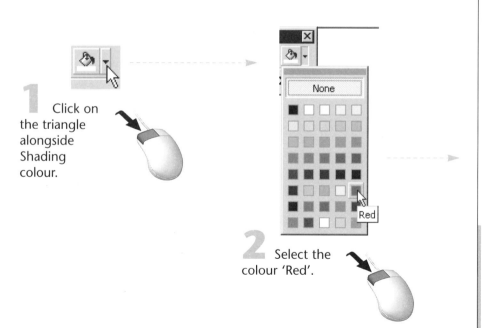

1 Click on the triangle alongside Shading colour.

2 Select the colour 'Red'.

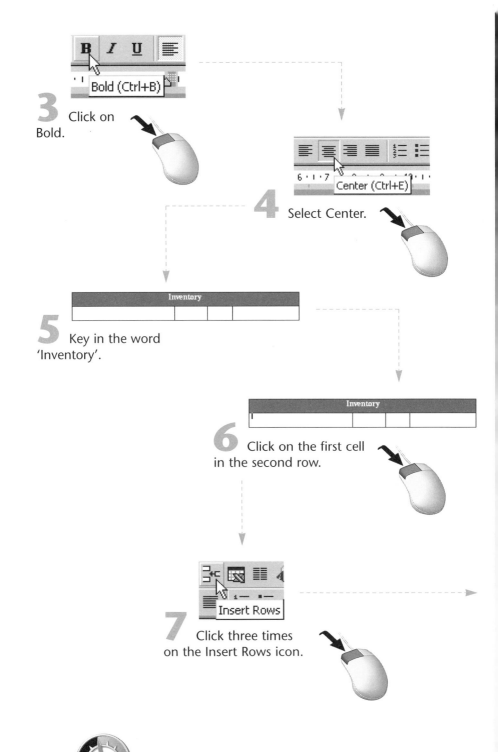

3 Click on Bold.

4 Select Center.

5 Key in the word 'Inventory'.

6 Click on the first cell in the second row.

7 Click three times on the Insert Rows icon.

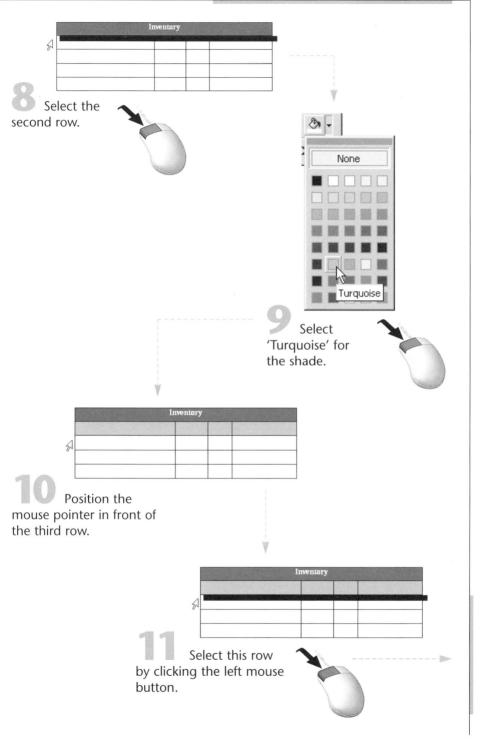

8 Select the second row.

9 Select 'Turquoise' for the shade.

10 Position the mouse pointer in front of the third row.

11 Select this row by clicking the left mouse button.

131

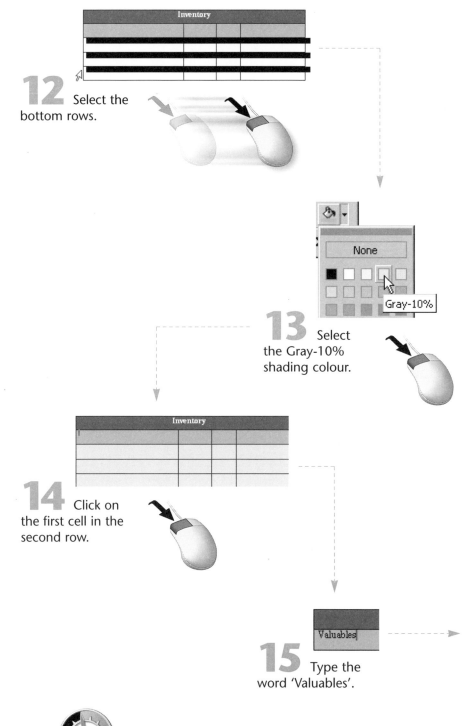

12 Select the
bottom rows.

None

Gray-10%

13 Select
the Gray-10%
shading colour.

Inventory

14 Click on
the first cell in the
second row.

Valuables

15 Type the
word 'Valuables'.

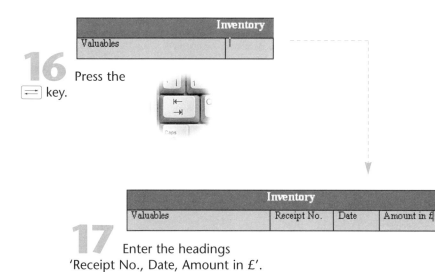

16 Press the ⇄ key.

17 Enter the headings 'Receipt No., Date, Amount in £'.

Splitting a table

Inventory			
Valuables	Receipt No.	Date	Amount in £

We want a space between the first and second rows. How do we do this? The answer is to split the table.

Use the Table/Split Table menu command.

You must also tell Word that the second row, i.e. 'Valuables, Receipt No.' etc. is the table header – in other words, the heading. The advantage of this is that if your list of valuables goes over one page, the 'Valuables, Receipt No.' row will appear on the next page.

133

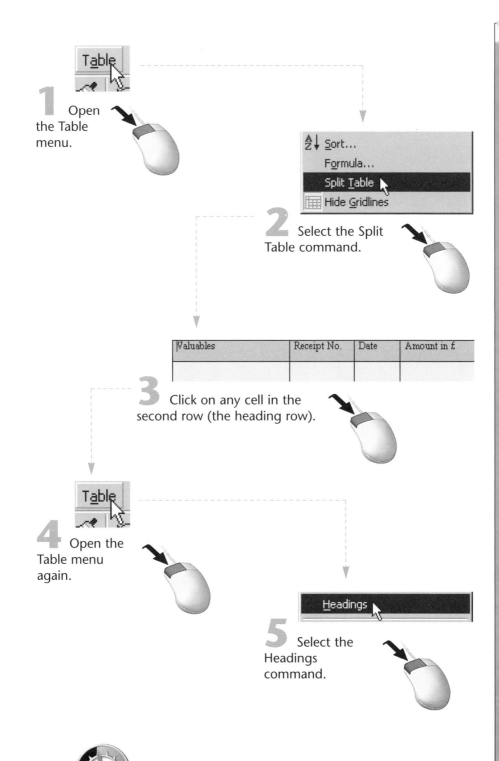

1 Open the Table menu.

Sort...
Formula...
Split Table
Hide Gridlines

2 Select the Split Table command.

Valuables	Receipt No.	Date	Amount in £

3 Click on any cell in the second row (the heading row).

4 Open the Table menu again.

Headings

5 Select the Headings command.

Entering text into a table

Key in the various details. Use the ⬅ key to move from one cell to the next. If you are in the last cell of the table and need another row, just press again on the ⬅ key. Word will create a new row.

Valuables	Receipt No.	Date	Amount in £
Stereo system	1	20.04.95	495.00

1 Enter the details.

Valuables	Receipt No.	Date	Amount in £
Stereo system	1	20.04.95	495.00

2 Press the ⬅-key.

Valuables	Receipt No.	Date	Amount in £
Stereo system	1	20.04.95	495.00
Television	2	23.12.95	425.00
Gold necklace	3	31.02.96	300.00

3 Complete the rows.

Valuables	Receipt No.	Date	Amount in £
Stereo system	1	20.04.95	495.00
Television	2	23.12.95	425.00
Gold necklace	3	31.02.96	300.00

4 Press the ⬅-key.

135

Inventory			
Valuables	Receipt No.	Date	Amount in £
Stereo system	1	20.04.95	495.00
Television	2	23.12.95	425.00
Gold necklace	3	31.02.96	300.00
Computer	4	02.01.97	970.00
Washing machine	5	10.01.97	500.00
Gold ring	6	20.09.97	833.00
Watch	7	21.09.97	1500.00
Total valuables			

 Fill in the table as above.

Deleting table gridlines

I am sure you will already have noticed the eraser on the Tables and Borders toolbar. Amazingly, you can actually use it to erase things. All you have to do is to click on the icon and the mouse pointer will change accordingly. Then click on the gridline which you want to get rid of in the table. Click again on the icon or press the $\boxed{\text{Esc}}$ key to cancel this function.

Select the Eraser.

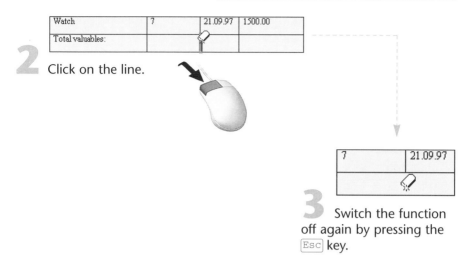

2 Click on the line.

3 Switch the function off again by pressing the `Esc` key.

Inserting borders

We've now got to add up our figures. We are going to highlight, almost 'frame', the cell where the end result is going to be. To do this, we use another type of line. Line Style gives you a choice. You then have to specify where this new line style is to appear. Outside Border gives you another choice. The highlighted lines show you where the new line will appear: left, right, above, below. In our case, we want to 'frame' the whole cell, so select the button showing a full border.

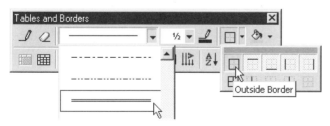

137

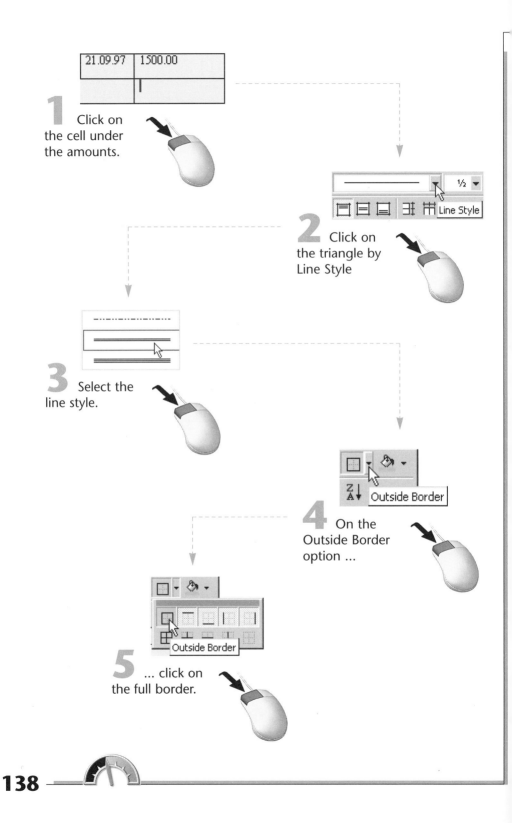

| 21.09.97 | 1500.00 |
| | |

1 Click on the cell under the amounts.

½

Line Style

2 Click on the triangle by Line Style

3 Select the line style.

Outside Border

4 On the Outside Border option ...

Outside Border

5 ... click on the full border.

Adding numbers

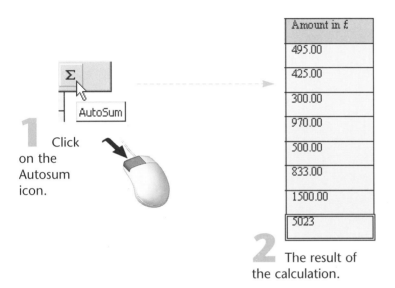

We are now going to add up the numbers in the cells. To do this, we use AutoSum. The cursor must be flashing in the last cell. As soon as you click on the AutoSum icon, Word adds up the cells above and enters the result in the bottom cell.

1 Click on the Autosum icon.

AutoSum

Amount in £
495.00
425.00
300.00
970.00
500.00
833.00
1500.00
5023

2 The result of the calculation.

Another calculation

It will not have escaped your notice that our result does not have a decimal point. As the figures do not have any values after the decimal point, Word does not show them. If a number is changed or a new one is entered, the calculation must be done again.

1500.00
5023

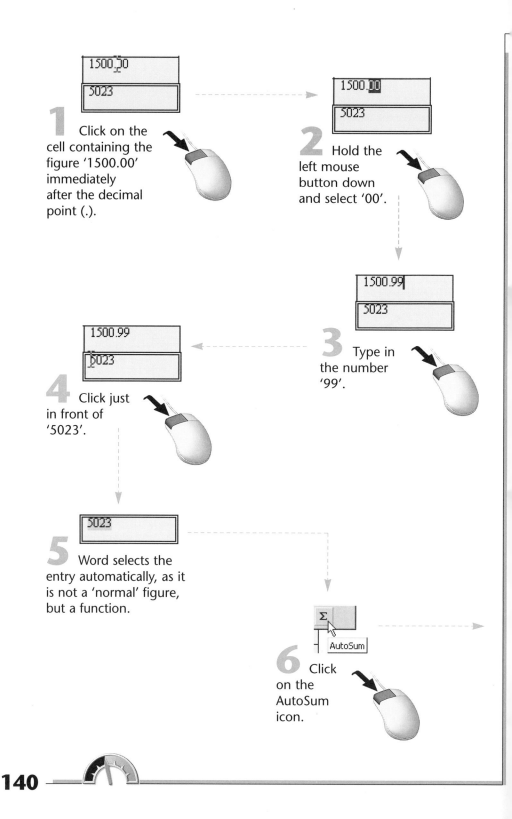

1 Click on the cell containing the figure '1500.00' immediately after the decimal point (.).

2 Hold the left mouse button down and select '00'.

3 Type in the number '99'.

4 Click just in front of '5023'.

5 Word selects the entry automatically, as it is not a 'normal' figure, but a function.

AutoSum

6 Click on the AutoSum icon.

Amount in £
495.00
425.00
300.00
970.00
500.00
833.00
1500.99
5023.99

7 The new result

Tables and Borders

8 Turn the Tables and Borders toolbar off.

Date	Amount in £
20.04.95	495.00
23.12.95	425.00
31.02.96	300.00
02.01.97	970.00
10.01.97	500.00
20.09.97	833.00
21.09.97	1500.99
	5023.99

9 Position the mouse pointer.

Date	Amount in £
20.04.95	495.00
23.12.95	425.00

10 Click on the left mouse button, hold it down...

141

Date	Amount in £
20.04.95	495.00
23.12.95	425.00
31.02.96	300.00
02.01.97	970.00
10.01.97	500.00
20.09.97	833.00
21.09.97	1500.99
	5023.99

11 ... and select the cells.

Align Right (Ctrl+R)

12 Click on the Right-align button.

Inventory			
Valuables	Receipt No.	Date	Amount in £
Stereo system	1	20.04.95	495.00
Television	2	23.12.95	425.00
Gold necklace	3	31.02.96	300.00
Computer	4	02.01.97	970.00
Washing machine	5	10.01.97	500.00
Gold ring	6	20.09.97	833.00
Watch	7	21.09.97	1500.99
Total valuables:			5023.99

13 Click either mouse button to remove the selection.

The Tables Trainer

Practice, practice, practice – tables give plenty of opportunity for it. The next few exercises will not only consolidate your knowledge, but will also teach you new ways of doing things.

More sums!

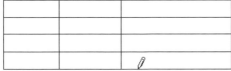

1 Draw the table using the Draw Table feature. If it does not work, insert a table using the Insert Table button on the standard toolbar.

Last name	First name	Amount paid in £
Apple	Adam	400
Summers	Eve	600

2 Enter these details into the table, and centre the contents of the third column for neatness.

Last name	First name	Amount paid in £
Apple	Adam	400
Summers	Eve	600

3 We want to add a shading colour to the table, changing the background. To do this, select the entire table.

None

Gray-25%

4 Now select a shading colour.

Last name	First name	Amount paid in £
Apple	Adam	400
Summers	Eve	600
		1000

5 It looks good in grey. But it's only a practice run, so you can of course choose any colour you like.

But now we're moving on to sums. Work out the result using the Autosum icon.

Last name	First name	Amount paid in £
Apple	Adam	400
Summers	Eve	600
		1000

6 Erase the unwanted lines.

Summers	Eve	

7 Perhaps you don't like the grey area which has been left behind. That is not a problem – we'll just remove it. Click inside this cell and ...

8 ... select None for the shading colour.

Behind bars?

Last name	First name	Amount paid in £
Apple	Adam	400
Summers	Eve	600
		1000

Last name	First name
Apple	Adam
Summers	Eve

If you see some fainter lines in your table, do not worry. Word has put them there. They will not appear when the document is printed.

Alternatively, you can actually get rid of the lines using the Table/Hide Gridlines menu command.

Creating tables using AutoFormat

We have already mentioned that you can also define the appearance of your table using the Table/Table AutoFormat menu command. There are lots more options to choose from here. Print Preview will show you what it will look like.

1 Place the cursor somewhere inside your table. This is the only way you can select the Table/Table AutoFormat menu option.

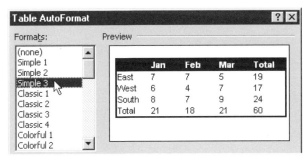

2 Select any format you wish.

6

Placing an order in writing

What's in this chapter?

'Who should pay, who ordered it?' We are going to order several items and list them in a standard way, one after the other, so that the supplier does not overlook anything either. The order letter includes

the item number, the item, quantity and order price.

Dear Sir or Madam

I would like to order the following items from you

Item No.	Item	Quantity	Unit Price in £
00001	Trousers, grey	50	20.00
4711	Blouse, red	50	13.33
0897	Socks, red	120	0.99
007	T-shirt, yellow	200	3.99
008	T-shirt, blue	400	3.00
009	T-shirt, black	100	2.99
1010	Pullover, yellow	10	9.99

Yours faithfully,

Pauline Harris

You already know:

You are going to learn:

Different types of tabs

By pressing the [⇥] key, you can move the cursor in bigger steps. This is not just quicker, but also saves you the trouble of pressing the [Space] bar umpteen times. Several terms are used in connection with tabs, such as 'Tab, Tab Stop or Tabulator Stop', but they all mean the same.

The default tabstops (i.e. the 'cursor jumps') in Word are set in centimetres (cm) as standard.

The default space between the tabs is 1.25 cm. You can also set the tabs for yourself. Selecting the Format/Tabs menu command opens up a dialog box. One of the options it displays is the Default tab stops option. Enter the required spacing here.

The ruler has to be the simplest and quickest way of setting tabs. This is why, at least for work where tabs will need to be set, the ruler should be permanently displayed (Menu command View/Ruler). To the left of the ruler you will see an 'L'.

Left Tab

This 'L' means that by clicking on the ruler, left-aligned tabs will be set for the moment. The text is aligned from left to right, as usual.

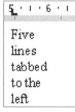

Five
lines
tabbed
to the
left

Center Tab

If you click again on the symbol, the respective tabs will change. The centred tab stop which now appears is set towards the middle of a text.

Five
lines
tabbed
to the
centre

Right Tab

The next, right-aligned tab stop aligns the text from right to left.

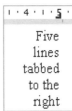

Five
lines
tabbed
to the
right

Decimal Tab

The last type, the decimal tab stop, is often used with figures. The decimal points of each set of figures will be aligned exactly.

7.77 pounds
£4.23
1,200.33
GBP 34.55
777.77028
£42,711.84
99,999.99

Setting a tab stop

This is very simple. Just move the mouse pointer on the ruler and click with the mouse button. The tab (tab stop) appears. To make it even easier, in this case you can press either the right or the left mouse button. If you now use the ⇥ key, you can make the cursor 'jump' right to the tab position.

Pauline·Harris¶

1 Type in the text.

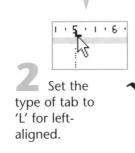

2 Set the type of tab to 'L' for left-aligned.

151

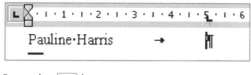

3 Press the ⏎ key.

Inserting the current date

Every letter needs a date. After all, both you and the recipient will want to know when you wrote this letter. So we insert the date. This is done by using the Insert/Date and Time menu command. Now you can choose what you want your date to look like. It can be shown numerically, '11.06.97' for example, or in words, 'Wednesday, 11th June 1997'.

Word enters the date, but it does something even better too. If you open the letter again the next day, to amend the order perhaps, the letter will show the previous date. So you just instruct Word to update the date automatically. All you have to do is to select the Update automatically checkbox in the Date and Time dialog box. Whenever you open this letter again, whether it's tomorrow, next week or next year, the current date will always be shown, provided, of course, that your computer is 'ticking' right, i.e. has the right date. Click OK to confirm your instructions, and Word will insert the date. If you now click with the mouse pointer in front of the date which has been inserted, it will be selected with a grey box. This means that this is no 'ordinary' date, but a field with an updating function.

How times are changing

Your computer should always be up-to-date with regard to the date or time. As a Windows 95 or Windows NT user, you are always kept informed of what's what. You can see it at the bottom on the task bar. Unless your computer is actually connected to a radio clock, there can, of course, be no guarantee that the time or date shown will be exactly right. Position the mouse pointer on the time display, then double-click. Set the correct date and time in the Date and Time dialog box and click on the Accept and OK buttons to confirm.

Windows 95 automatically takes into account the change from summer to winter time and vice-versa.

But now back to the task in hand!

We are going to enter the current date and tell Word that this should be updated each time the document is opened.

153

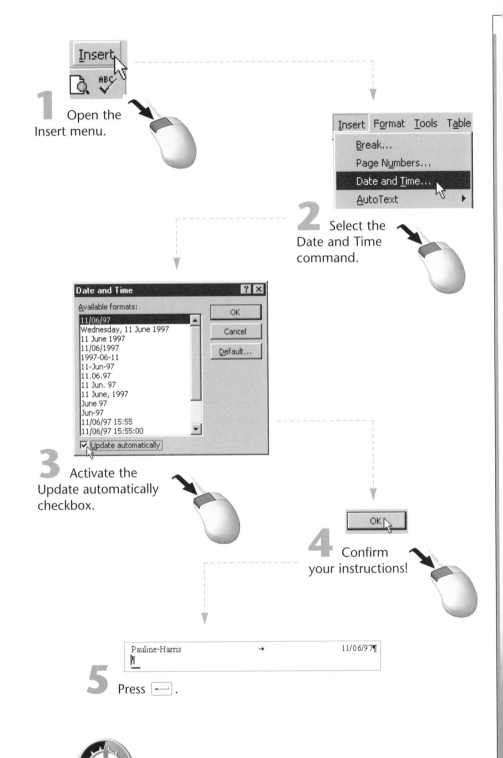

1 Open the Insert menu.

Insert Format Tools Table
- Break...
- Page Numbers...
- Date and Time...
- AutoText ▶

2 Select the Date and Time command.

Date and Time

A̲vailable formats:

- 11/06/97
- Wednesday, 11 June 1997
- 11 June 1997
- 11/06/1997
- 1997-06-11
- 11-Jun-97
- 11.06.97
- 11 Jun. 97
- 11 June, 1997
- June 97
- Jun-97
- 11/06/97 15:55
- 11/06/97 15:55:00

OK
Cancel
Default...

☑ U̲pdate automatically

3 Activate the Update automatically checkbox.

OK

4 Confirm your instructions!

Pauline·Harris → 11/06/97¶

5 Press ⏎ .

Setting tabs

When you press the [⇥] key, the cursor 'jumps' on a bit. You can control the length of the jump by setting the tabs on the ruler. This will position the cursor directly on this tab. Just select the position on the ruler and click with the left mouse button. If you hold it down, a vertical broken line will appear in the document. Release the mouse button again and the tab you selected will have been set on the ruler.

TIP

You can set tabs using either the left or the right mouse button.

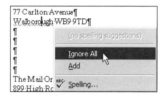

Remember that Word often underlines proper names, as it does not generally recognise them. You can leave it like that or alternatively, if it disturbs you, you can switch the lines off altogether by selecting Ignore All in the Spelling and Grammar page of the Tools/Options menu.

TIP

The subject line used always to start with the word 'Concerning' or 'Re'. This is not so common nowadays. As a rule, the subject line is now emphasised by using a larger font or bold.

We are now going to emphasise the subject of our 'order' letter.

1 Type in the text.

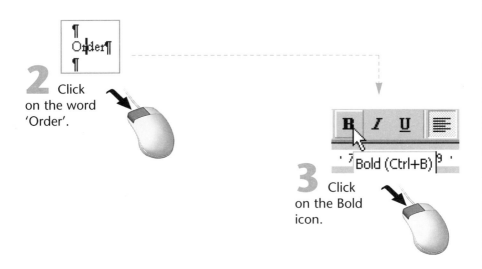

2 Click on the word 'Order'.

3 Click on the Bold icon.

Bold (Ctrl+B)

When setting tabs, it is important that the cursor is positioned in the right line. The tab stops apply only for those lines for which they have been defined. If you press ⏎ afterwards, the tab stops will be carried forward into the following line.

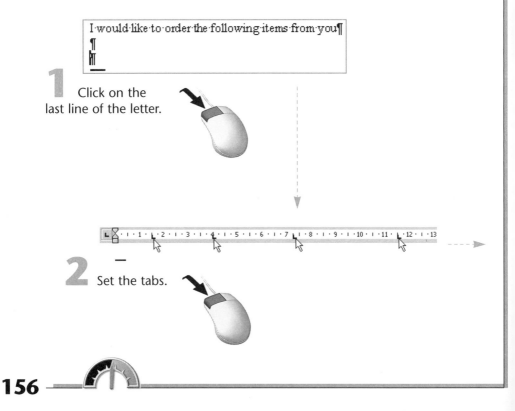

1 Click on the last line of the letter.

2 Set the tabs.

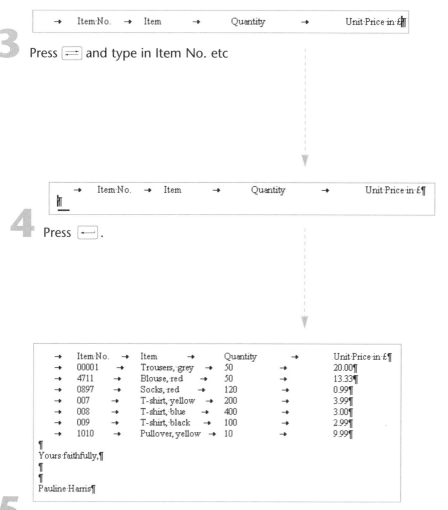

3 Press ⇄ and type in Item No. etc

4 Press ⏎ .

5 Enter the text above.

Editing tables

We can emphasise the heading of our little table slightly by setting it in bold. To do this, we have to select the row and click on the relevant icon.

157

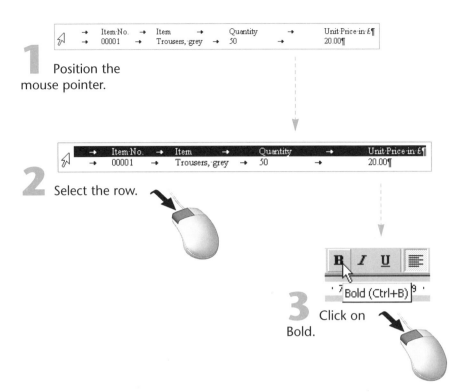

1 Position the
mouse pointer.

2 Select the row.

3 Click on
Bold.

Bold (Ctrl+B)

Selecting rows

We want to change the tabs in the other rows. So that Word makes
all the changes to the tabs at the same time in all the rows, we must
first select the rows. First select one row, click with the left mouse
button and hold it down. Then drag the mouse down onto the other
rows.

| | → | 00001 | → | Trousers, grey | → | 50 | → | 20.00¶ |
| | → | 4711 | → | Blouse, red | → | 50 | → | 13.33¶ |

1 Position the
mouse pointer.

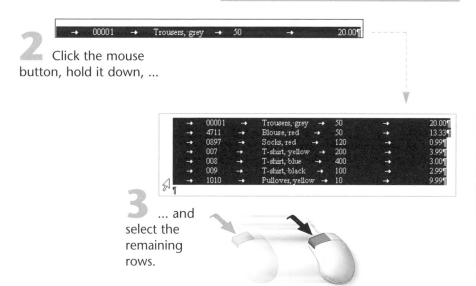

2 Click the mouse
button, hold it down, ...

3 ... and
select the
remaining
rows.

Changing the type of tabs

The present alignment is not neat enough. The alignment under
'Item No.' and 'Quantity' looks decidedly untidy. Setting right-
aligned tabs would definitely make for a clearer layout. So we are
going to change the type of tab to right-aligned.

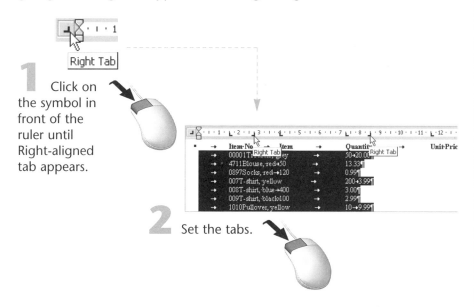

1 Click on
the symbol in
front of the
ruler until
Right-aligned
tab appears.

2 Set the tabs.

159

Deleting tabs

Our table now looks rather chaotic. But don't worry – it will change! All you need do is delete the tab stops that are not needed – in other words, the two left-aligned tabs in our example.

Getting rid of tabs is extremely easy. Just click on the relevant tab stop, hold the mouse button down and drag into the white area, i.e. into the document area. Release the mouse button, and the tab stop has disappeared.

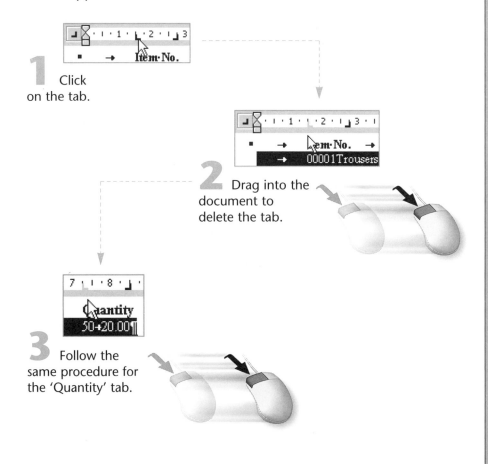

1 Click on the tab.

2 Drag into the document to delete the tab.

3 Follow the same procedure for the 'Quantity' tab.

The decimal tab

Decimal tabs would definitely be the best option for the 'Unit Price in £' column, as these would be set by the decimal point in the amount. In this way, all the decimal points would be neatly aligned one below the other in a vertical line.

It is easy to delete the left-aligned tab stop.

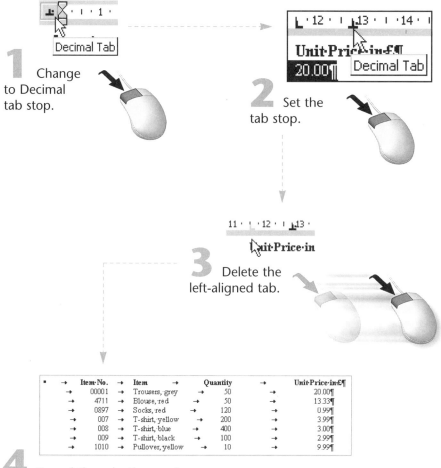

1 Change to Decimal tab stop.

2 Set the tab stop.

3 Delete the left-aligned tab.

4 Cancel the selection again by clicking either mouse button.

Moving tabs

If you don't like the position of a tab, move it. To do this, click on the tab and hold the mouse button down while you move it to a new position. We would like to move the 'Item No.' heading slightly to the right. This applies to only one row. All you have to do is to put the cursor into this row or select it.

At the same time, we will also underline the headings.

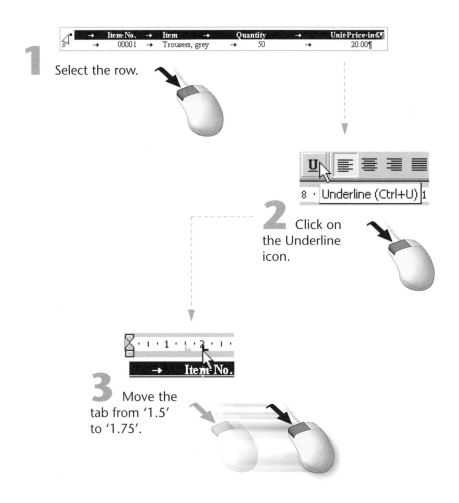

1 Select the row.

2 Click on the Underline icon.

3 Move the tab from '1.5' to '1.75'.

Getting rid of unwanted underlining

The underlining in front of 'Item No.' now looks rather out-of-place and we therefore want to get rid of it. First, select the unwanted underlining. Then select the Underline icon or press the [Ctrl] + [Space] bar keyboard shortcut. If you choose the keyboard shortcut, remember to hold the [Ctrl] key down while pressing the [Space] bar, then release both. The underlining will be deleted.

To round off this chapter, we will print the order letter.

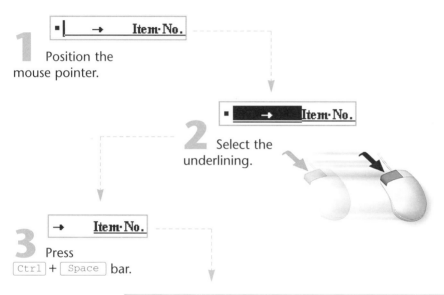

1 Position the
mouse pointer.

2 Select the
underlining.

3 Press
[Ctrl] + [Space] bar.

Dear Sir or Madam

I would like to order the following items from you

Item No.	Item	Quantity	Unit Price in £
00001	Trousers, grey	50	20.00
4711	Blouse, red	50	13.33
0897	Socks, red	120	0.99
007	T-shirt, yellow	200	3.99
008	T-shirt, blue	400	3.00
009	T-shirt, black	100	2.99
1010	Pullover, yellow	10	9.99

Yours faithfully,

Pauline Harris

Print (Brother HL-730 series) (Ctrl+P)

4 Check the text, before
printing it out.

The Word Trainer

The following exercises will not only consolidate your knowledge, they will also broaden it. For example, if you are working with tabs, you cannot use the Sort feature. You can, however, convert the text to a table.

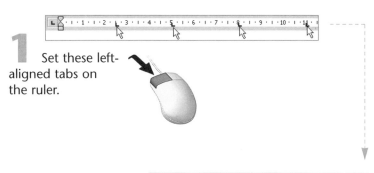

1 Set these left-aligned tabs on the ruler.

Last Name	First Name	Nickname	Birthday	Hobbies
Anderson	James	Jumbo	03.08.62	Rowing
Williams	George	Billy	07.07.32	Bowling
Holland	Daniel	Brains	23.11.74	Walking
Barker	Wendy	Wen	14.09.79	Dancing

2 Enter the table as shown here.

3 Select the table, so that Word knows what it should be editing. Just position the cursor in front of the first row. The mouse pointer will change the direction in which it is pointing. Then click once on the left mouse button and drag the selection downwards over the other rows.

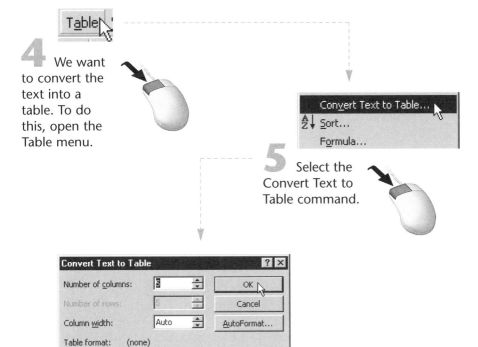

4 We want to convert the text into a table. To do this, open the Table menu.

5 Select the Convert Text to Table command.

6 Word will tell you how big the table is going to look. You can see from the entry, Number of columns '5', that the table has five columns. Click on OK.

Last Name	First Name	Nickname	Birthday	Hobbies
Anderson	James	Jumbo	03.08.62	Rowing
Williams	George	Billy	07.07.32	Bowling
Holland	Daniel	Brains	23.11.74	Walking
Barker	Wendy	Wen	14.09.79	Dancing

Word converts the previous text into a table, which you can now edit – for example, sort it. If you want to convert the table back into ordinary text again, place the cursor in the table, then you can select the reverse command, Convert Table to Text, in the Table menu.

165

7

Word, the bill please!

What's in this chapter?

Everybody needs money to live on, and anyone who has provided a service expects to get paid. But first an invoice has to be made out. So we are going to design an invoice form. Word can be helpful in determining the individual amounts. A calculating function is 'hidden' in the program and we can tie it in with the menu. If we want our money paid into the bank, we can quote our bank details at the bottom of the invoice.

You already know:

You are going to learn:

167

Headers and Footers

A letter always consists of the letter text; a person consists of head, body, feet and everything else in between. The letter text is the body, but in our document you will also find a head and a foot. The purpose of these zones is to be able to position texts at the top and/or bottom of the page. As you know from your own experience, the company logo or company name is at the top. In the case of an invoice, it is obviously a good idea to quote the bank details at the bottom of the page.

You can define headers and footers using the View/Header and Footer menu option.

A new toolbar, the Header and Footer toolbar, will be opened on the screen. You will also notice a broken-lined box. Enter the text for the header here.

Header

We now want to enter our instructions in the header, before we format it a little for appearance's sake. We are going to change the font size, select bold and centre everything.

1 Open the View menu.

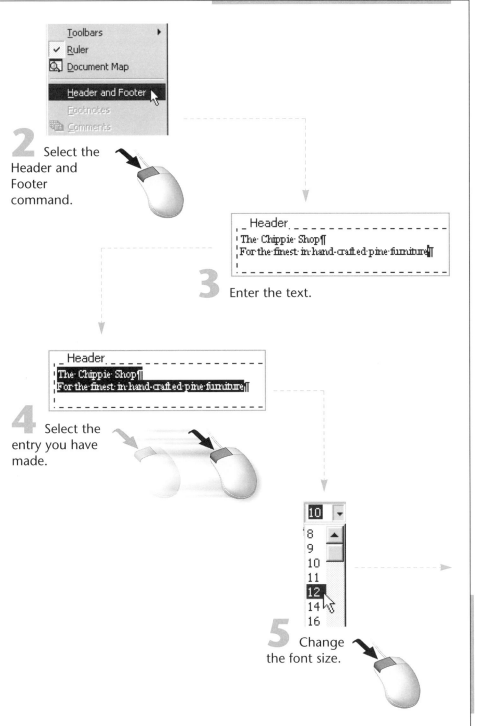

Toolbars
✓ Ruler
Document Map
Header and Footer
Footnotes
Comments

2 Select the Header and Footer command.

Header
The Chippie Shop¶
For the finest in hand-crafted pine furniture¶

3 Enter the text.

Header
The Chippie Shop¶
For the finest in hand-crafted pine furniture¶

4 Select the entry you have made.

10 ▾
8
9
10
11
12
14
16

5 Change the font size.

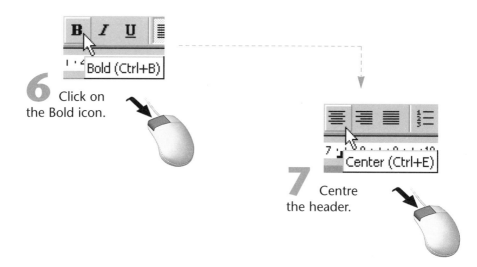

6 Click on the Bold icon.

7 Centre the header.

Footers

Head and foot go 'hand in hand' – so you will find the footer right at the bottom of the page. In our example, we are going to give our bank details here. The next icon shown in the Header and Footer toolbar is important for us, as it switches between the header and footer. If you click on this icon now, you will find that you are no longer in the header, but are in the footer.

Once you have entered the footer text, centre it and format it in Bold. Complete your entries by selecting the Close button.

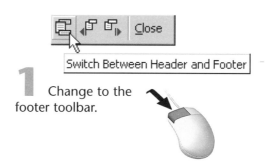

1 Change to the footer toolbar.

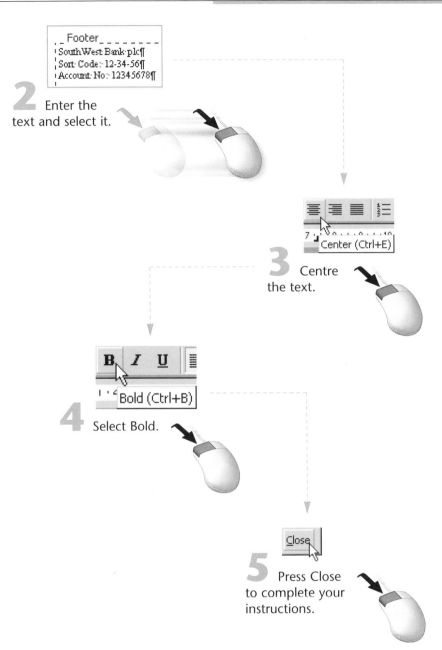

Footer
SouthWest Bank plc¶
Sort Code: 12-34-56¶
Account No: 12345678¶

2 Enter the text and select it.

Center (Ctrl+E)

3 Centre the text.

Bold (Ctrl+B)

4 Select Bold.

Close

5 Press Close to complete your instructions.

171

Different views

In Word, there are different 'views'. This has nothing to do with opinions, but with the way the document is displayed. You will find the various display options in the View menu. Normal View and Page Layout are the important ones for you as a beginner.

In what ways are these two views different? Page Layout resembles the printed page very closely, because you can see the text of the headers and footers. You can also see page numbers (which we will cover in a later chapter). The document will appear on the screen as shown here. A ruler is displayed not only at the top, but also on the left.

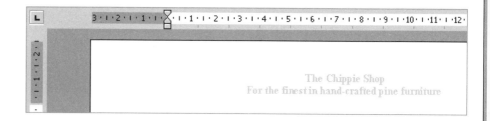

The Chippie Shop
For the finest in hand-crafted pine furniture

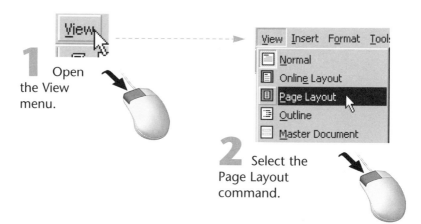

1 Open the View menu.

View Insert Format Tool
- Normal
- Online Layout
- Page Layout
- Outline
- Master Document

2 Select the Page Layout command.

Sender and recipient

We are going to type in the sender's details. If you follow the carriage returns shown here exactly, the letter will fit in a window envelope, as long as you fold it correctly. The windows of these envelopes also show the sender immediately alongside the recipient. This is what we want to do here.

We are therefore going to type in the sender's details in a line above the recipient. Leave two spaces (Space bar) between each section of the address.

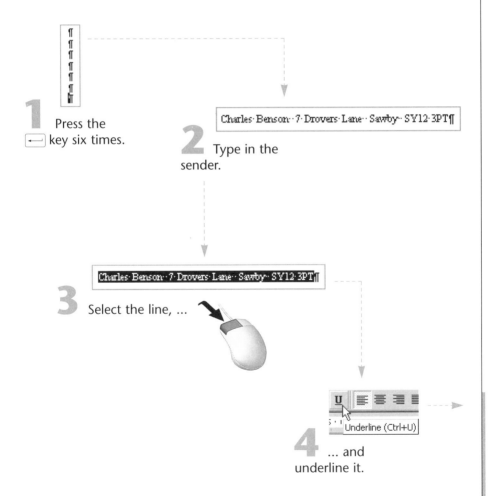

1 Press the
⟵ key six times.

2 Type in the
sender.

Charles·Benson··7·Drovers·Lane··Sawby··SY12·3PT¶

3 Select the line, …

Charles·Benson··7·Drovers·Lane··Sawby··SY12·3PT¶

U ≣ ≣ ≣ ≣
Underline (Ctrl+U)

4 … and
underline it.

Charles·Benson···7·Drovers·Lane···Sawby··SY12·3PT¶
¶
Mr·Harold·Benson¶
815·Park·Drive¶
Sawby··SY1·2BA¶

5 Type in the recipient details
for our invoice.

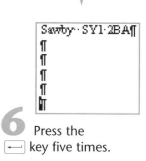

6 Press the
⬅ key five times.

The subject heading

Every letter needs a subject heading. The invoice number is of course
shown in an invoice. It has to be quoted when payments are made.
To make sure it doesn't get overlooked, we are going to format it in
Bold.

But this time, we are going to do it differently, so that you get to
know this way too. First, you click on the icon and only then do you
write the text. To cancel Bold again, click on the icon once again
after writing the text. From then on, your text will continue to be
written in 'normal' font.

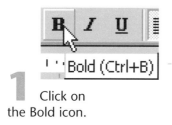

1 Click on
the Bold icon.

Invoice·No·:·07/1001¶

2 Enter your text.

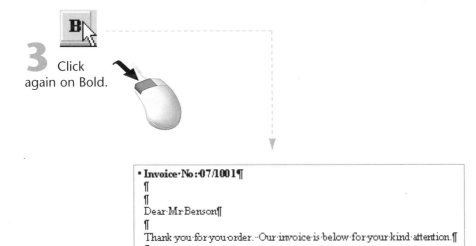

3 Click
again on Bold.

• Invoice·No:·07/1001¶
¶
¶
Dear·Mr·Benson¶
¶
Thank·you·for·you·order.··Our·invoice·is·below·for·your·kind·attention.¶
¶
¶

4 Continue writing the text. Note the position of
the cursor. Position your cursor in the same place.

Setting tabs

The next steps will teach you how to set the position of the tabs.
This will enable us to create a little table to show the individual
details clearly in our invoice, so that the reader can immediately see
what we are wanting money for.

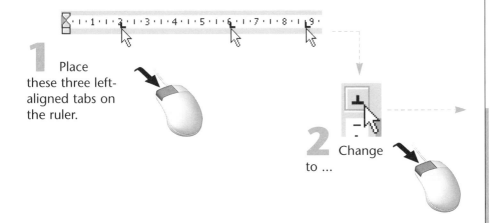

1 Place
these three left-
aligned tabs on
the ruler.

2 Change
to ...

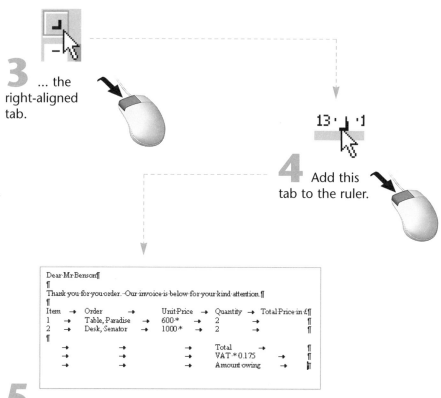

3 ... the right-aligned tab.

4 Add this tab to the ruler.

Dear·Mr·Benson¶
¶
Thank·you·for·you·order.··Our·invoice·is·below·for·your·kind·attention.¶
¶
Item → Order → UnitPrice → Quantity → TotalPrice·in·£¶
1 → Table,·Paradise → 600·* → 2 → ¶
2 → Desk,·Senator → 1000·* → 2 → ¶
¶
→ → → Total → ¶
→ → → VAT·*·0.175 → ¶
→ → → Amount·owing → ¶

5 Type in the invoice entries as above.

Customised menus

What's the point of writing an invoice, if we can't calculate anything on it? Word does in fact have the necessary functions, but they are not in any menu. At least, not yet! It is possible to add new commands to menus. In fact, Word can even calculate.

If you select the Commands tab from the Tools/Customize menu, you will see several categories. If you select Tools, you will find the function we require, which you can use to calculate in Word.

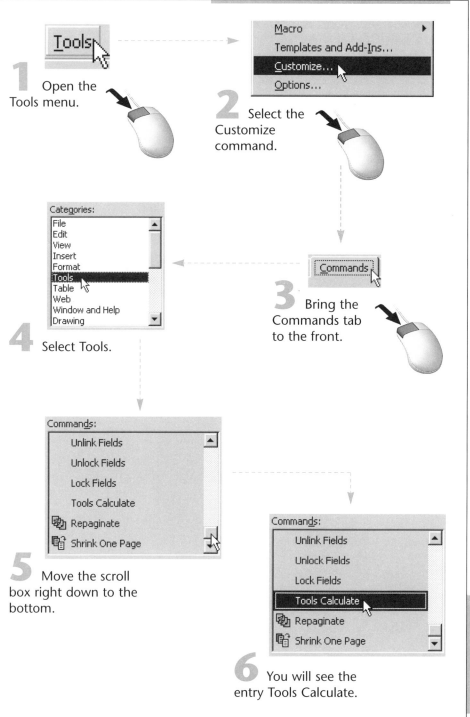

Macro ▸
Templates and Add-Ins...
Customize...
Options...

1 Open the
Tools menu.

2 Select the
Customize
command.

Categories:
File
Edit
View
Insert
Format
Tools
Table
Web
Window and Help
Drawing

Commands

3 Bring the
Commands tab
to the front.

4 Select Tools.

Commands:
Unlink Fields
Unlock Fields
Lock Fields
Tools Calculate
Repaginate
Shrink One Page

5 Move the scroll
box right down to the
bottom.

Commands:
Unlink Fields
Unlock Fields
Lock Fields
Tools Calculate
Repaginate
Shrink One Page

6 You will see the
entry Tools Calculate.

177

Once we have found the desired function, it just has to be inserted into a particular Menu. We are going to use the Tools menu. The Customize dialog box is still open on the screen. You are now going to open the Tools menu. The Customize dialog will stay open as you do it. If necessary, move the dialog so that you can see both the menu and the dialog box. With the mouse button pressed down, drag the Tools Calculate entry from the dialog box into the menu.

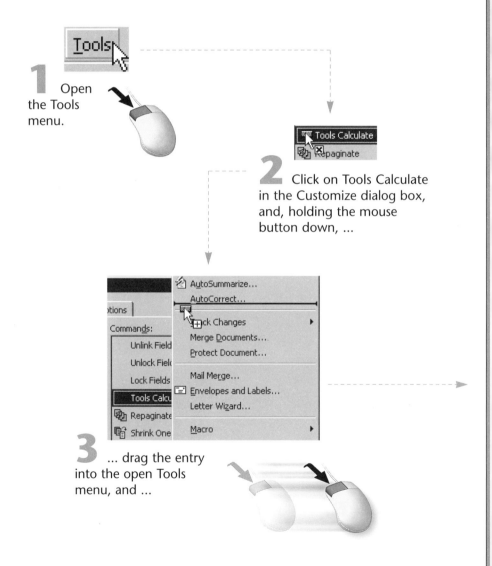

1 Open the Tools menu.

2 Click on Tools Calculate in the Customize dialog box, and, holding the mouse button down, ...

3 ... drag the entry into the open Tools menu, and ...

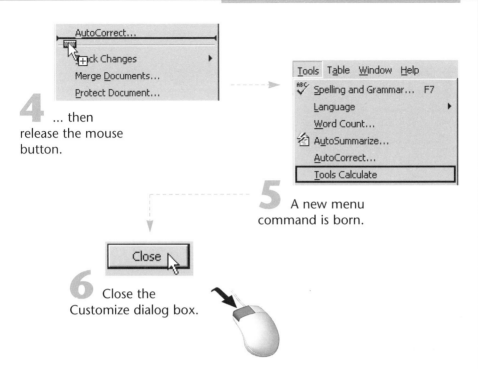

4 ... then release the mouse button.

5 A new menu command is born.

6 Close the Customize dialog box.

Calculating with Word

Now we could actually calculate, if we only knew how. If you open the Tools menu, however, you cannot carry out the calculation function, as the relevant menu option cannot be selected. So that Word knows what it should calculate, an area has to be selected. In our example, we would like to determine the final price. To do this,

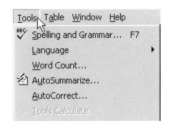

we select 'Unit Price' and 'Number of Items'. The '*' symbol tells Word that it should multiply. When you have selected the headings, simply select the Tools/Calculate Tools menu command. Nothing much seems to be actually happening on the screen, but take a closer look! Right at the bottom in the status bar, you will find the

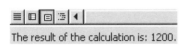

result. You have to move the cursor to the place where the result is to be inserted. Click on the Paste icon in the standard toolbar.

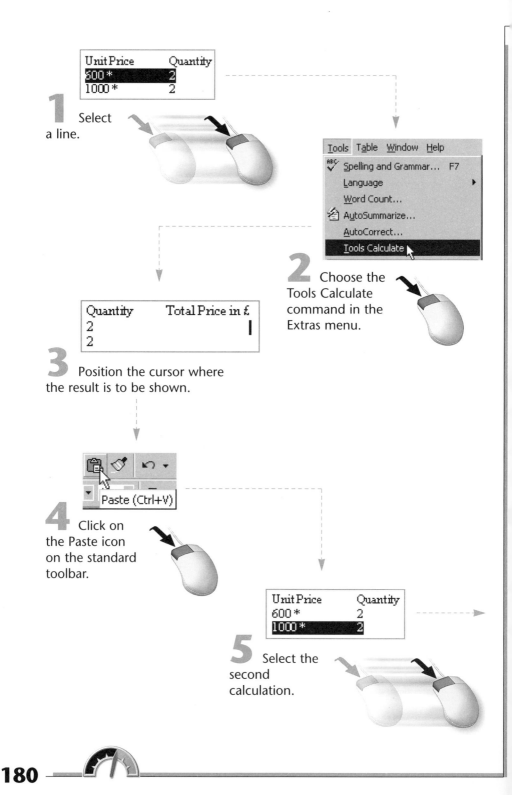

1 Select
a line.

Unit Price	Quantity
600 *	2
1000 *	2

Tools Table Window Help
- ABC Spelling and Grammar... F7
- Language ▸
- Word Count...
- AutoSummarize...
- AutoCorrect...
- Tools Calculate

2 Choose the
Tools Calculate
command in the
Extras menu.

Quantity	Total Price in £
2	
2	

3 Position the cursor where
the result is to be shown.

Paste (Ctrl+V)

4 Click on
the Paste icon
on the standard
toolbar.

Unit Price	Quantity
600 *	2
1000 *	2

5 Select the
second
calculation.

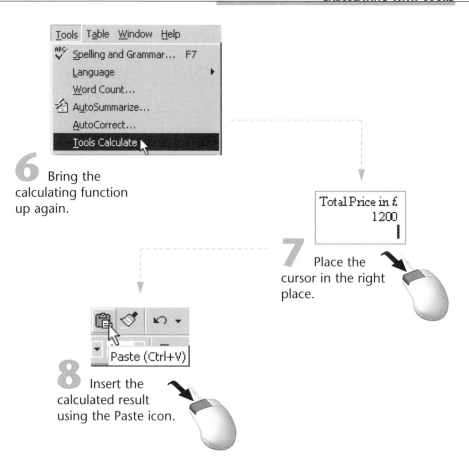

6 Bring the calculating function up again.

7 Place the cursor in the right place.

8 Insert the calculated result using the Paste icon.

Addition

Of course, we now want to add up the two individual entries, but we do not have to enter any '+' sign, as Word adds up the figures automatically if no particular calculation has been specified.

Item	Order	Unit Price	Quantity	Total Price in £
1	Table, Paradise	600 *	2	1200
2	Desk, Senator	1000 *	2	2000

181

As we already know, the terms must first be selected. But if we do that now, a problem arises. Word selects all of the second row and would therefore take every figure into consideration. That would be wrong!

We want to add only the two figures in the 'Total Price in £' column. There is a trick we can use to do this. Click in front of the first number. Press the $\boxed{\text{Alt}}$ key and keep it pressed down. Now select both figures using the mouse.

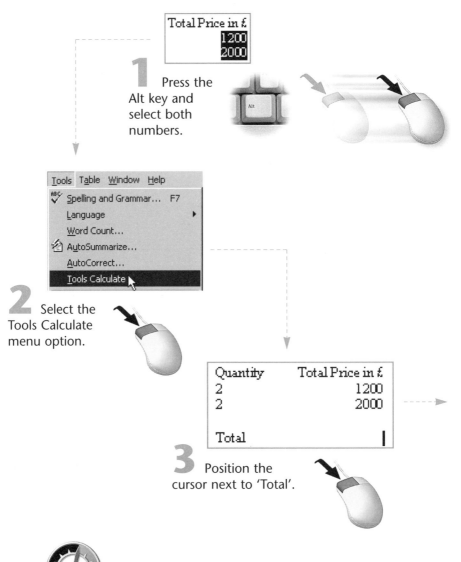

Total Price in £
1200
2000

1 Press the Alt key and select both numbers.

Tools	Table	Window	Help
✓	Spelling and Grammar...	F7
	Language	▶
	Word Count...	
	AutoSummarize...	
	AutoCorrect...	
	Tools Calculate	

2 Select the Tools Calculate menu option.

Quantity	Total Price in £
2	1200
2	2000
Total	

3 Position the cursor next to 'Total'.

4 Insert the result using the Paste button.

Multiplication

The VAT amount also has to be calculated, and unless the government has changed things without warning, it should still be 17.5%. To work this out, you calculate 17.5% of the net amount – £3,200 in our case.

The next few steps will prove once and for all that Word is not a fully fledged pocket calculator. It is a word processing program. For invoices, you would normally use table calculation programs such as Excel. It can, however, still be done with Word, but not so smartly. In this case, Excel is the Rolls Royce, while Word is more of a 2 CV. But both will get you there in the end.

To calculate 17.5% of £3,200, we multiply by 0.175.

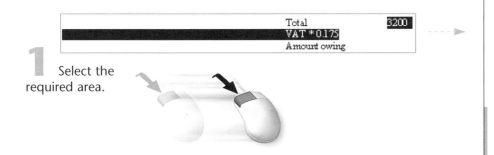

1 Select the required area.

183

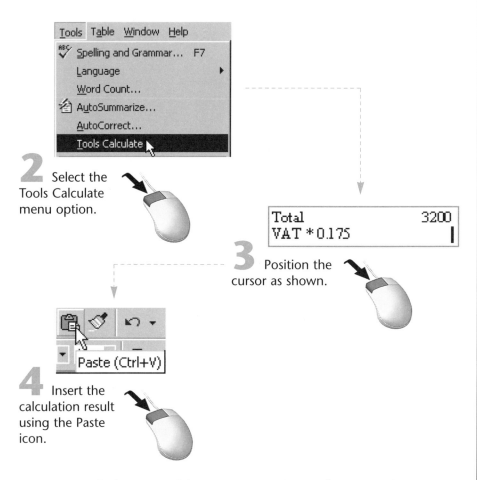

2 Select the Tools Calculate menu option.

3 Position the cursor as shown.

Total   3200
VAT $* 0.175$

4 Insert the calculation result using the Paste icon.

Now we again have to add two amounts in a column. We have already done this once, so it provides excellent consolidation practice for you and more work for the author!

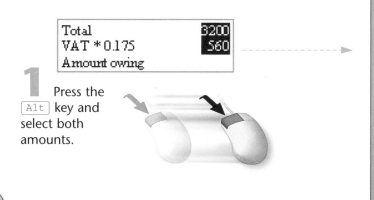

Total   3200
VAT $* 0.175$ 560
Amount owing

1 Press the [Alt] key and select both amounts.

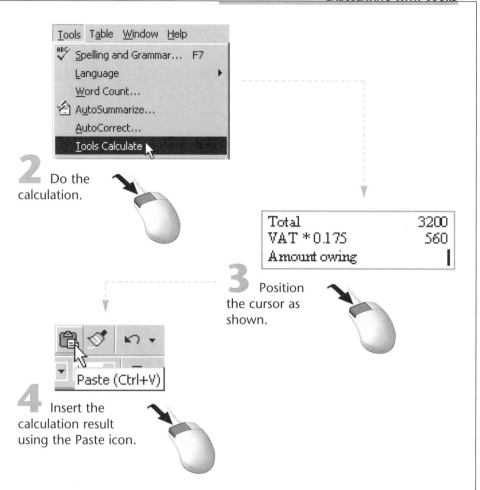

2 Do the calculation.

Total   3200
VAT * 0.175   560
Amount owing |

3 Position the cursor as shown.

Paste (Ctrl+V)

4 Insert the calculation result using the Paste icon.

The bill, please!

With Word, you can carry out a wide variety of calculations. The signs you need to do this are shown below:

Type of calculation	Signs
Addition	+ (or do not enter any sign)
Subtraction	–
Multiplication	*
Division	/

185

Deleting menu options

And so our invoice is now complete, but if you can add menu options, such as Tools Calculate, then you can surely also take them away again.

All you need do is open the Customize dialog box and the Tools menu at the same time. Then simply drag the command from the menu into the dialog box, and the entry is deleted.

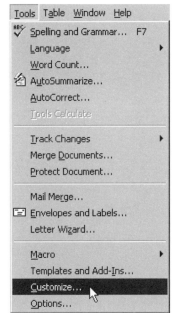

1 Open the Customize dialog box using Tools/Customize

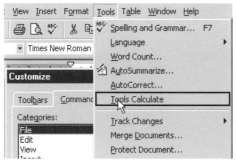

2 Select the Tools Calculate
menu option. Hold the mouse
button down, ...

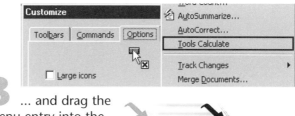

3 ... and drag the
menu entry into the
Customize dialog box.

The Word Trainer

In this exercise, we are going to set tabs and do a few sums with the
help of the Tools Calculate menu option.

1 Set the tabs. Select the tab stop as
shown in the diagram.

• Product	→	Quantity	→	X	→	Unit Price	→	=	→	Total Price ¶
Screws	→	600	→	*	→	0.50	→	=	→	¶
Nails	→	500	→	*	→	0.20	→	=	→	¶
• Tacks	→	500	→	*	→	0.20	→	=	→	¶
¶										
→		Net	→	→		→			→	¶
→		VAT	→	*	→	0.175	→	=	→	¶
→	Invoice·Amount	→		→		→		=	→	¶

2 Now enter the text. Press the ⏎ key as shown above.

Quantity	X	Unit Price	=	Total Price
600	*	0.50	=	300
500	*	0.20	=	100
500	*	0.20	=	100

3 Work out 'Number*Unit Price', and insert the result.

Total Price
300
100
100
500

4 Work out the net amount. Position the cursor in front of the figure '300', and then hold the Alt key and select the individual numbers using the mouse.

Net				500
VAT	*	0.175	=	87.5

5 How much does the government get? Calculate the amount of VAT. But be careful! The equals sign (=) must not be selected, as otherwise the calculation won't work.

6 Work out the invoice amount.

The calculation is finished, and this is what it looks like!

Product	Quantity	X	Unit Price	=	Total Price
Screws	600	*	0.50	=	300
Nails	500	*	0.20	=	100
Tacks	500	*	0.20	=	100
	Net				500
	VAT	*	0.175	=	87.5
	Invoice Amount			=	587.5

What's in
this chapter?

It pays to advertise. Many of us choose to
change jobs to improve our employment
prospects (and some of us, unfortunately, find
ourselves forced to do so). The first hurdle in
finding new employment is the written job
application. Your covering letter will invariably
contain standard phrases. Instead of writing
them out each time you apply for a job, why
not simply write them once and store them
away so you have them to hand when you next
need them? This will not
only save you time, but
will also enable you to
react quickly to adverts
in the job pages. This
chapter is about
getting Word to do
things automatically,
using the
AutoComplete,
AutoText and
AutoCorrect
facilities.

John Brown
156 Silver Street
Greenford GR2 1JS

Smith & Co.
345 Mill Street
Cottonham CO5 4DB

Re: Your job advertisement in the Commercial Times

Dear Sirs,

I read your job advertisement with great interest. The tasks that you describe sound very interesting and
I am looking for a new challenge in my career.

I have been working as a production engineer for two years. During this time I have added to my
knowledge by taking an Open University course.

I would be very pleased to support my application by attending an interview.

Yours faithfully,

John Brown

You already know:

You are going to learn:

AutoComplete

The words in the yellow boxes are called 'tips'.

Do you get fed up with typing the same old phrases? If so, we've got some good news for you! Word can

help. Perhaps you've already noticed that when you're entering text, Word will sometimes show you a suggestion. For example, this happens when you type one of the days of the week. If you type 'Mond', Word suggests 'Monday'.

You can accept this suggestion by pressing the ⮐ key. The same applies to all the days of the week. Word also offers you this facility for the longer names of months such as January, February and August. When you write today's date, you will also be shown a tip.

Other words have already been compiled for use in this way. You can find them by choosing the AutoCorrect command from the Tools menu and clicking on the AutoText tab.

You can also store your own words and phrases here. These could be your name or particularly long words such as 'antidisestablishmentarianism'. You only need to type these in once for them to be stored away as a tip.

In our example we have the name 'John Brown'. There are two slightly different ways that you can add this name to your AutoText list: either follow the six steps

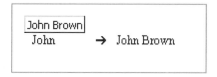

below exactly; or type the name into your document and select it, and then follow the routine below missing out steps 3 and 4.

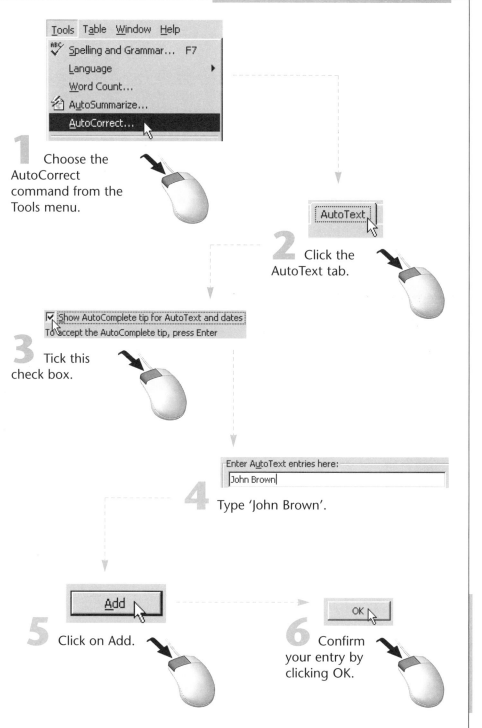

Tools Table Window Help

ABC Spelling and Grammar... F7
Language ▶
Word Count...
AutoSummarize...
AutoCorrect...

1 Choose the AutoCorrect command from the Tools menu.

AutoText

2 Click the AutoText tab.

☑ Show AutoComplete tip for AutoText and dates
To accept the AutoComplete tip, press Enter

3 Tick this check box.

Enter AutoText entries here:
John Brown

4 Type 'John Brown'.

Add

5 Click on Add.

OK

6 Confirm your entry by clicking OK.

193

Removing a tip

You can remove a tip from the dialog box by selecting it and clicking the Delete button.

Inserting a tip

After you've stored away 'John Brown', try typing the name and see what happens. As soon as you've written 'John', the yellow tip box suggests the rest of the name. Now press the ⟵ key and Word completes the name for you.

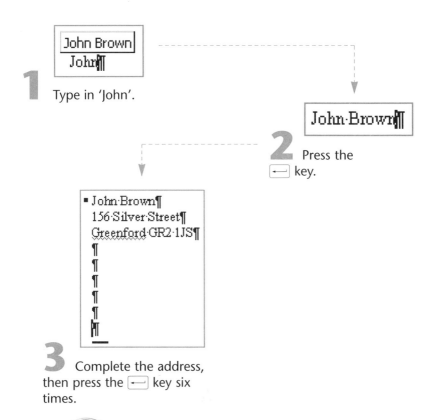

1 Type in 'John'.

2 Press the ⟵ key.

3 Complete the address, then press the ⟵ key six times.

AutoText or AutoCorrect?

That is the question! In Word 97 you can type in standard phrases or blocks of text once and insert them as required again and again.

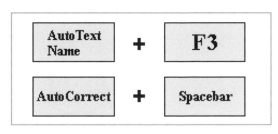

There are two ways of doing this, the first using AutoText. You save some text and give it a name. As soon as you write this name and press the F3 key, Word replaces it with the saved text.

The second way is to use AutoCorrect. The actual purpose of this facility is to enable you to list errors that you make regularly so that Word can automatically correct them (for example, if you type 'teh' instead of 'the').

You can also use AutoCorrect for a slightly different purpose. Blocks of text can also be stored away like this. You give the text a name, and when you write this name and press the Space bar, Word automatically inserts the saved text.

Which should you use, AutoText or AutoCorrect?

That entirely depends on you; we have shown you both ways. In practice, people tend to use AutoText for blocks of text and AutoCorrect for standard phrases such as 'Yours sincerely'.

Saving an AutoText entry

It does not matter whether you use upper or lower case letters when creating an AutoText entry.

In our example we will now save the sender's details as an AutoText entry. We will give it the name 'sdr'.

If you know how many blank lines will be needed after the sender's details, put these in too. This will ensure that the cursor always jumps to the correct position.

195

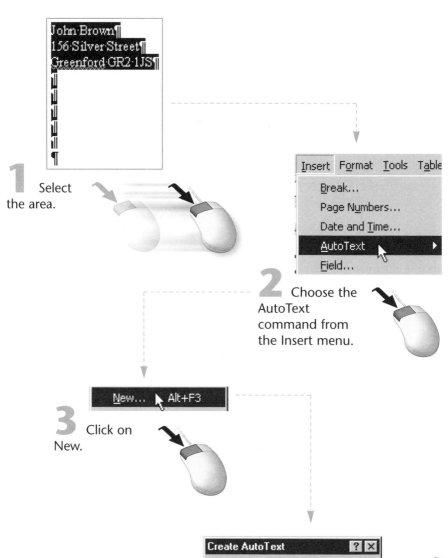

1 Select the area.

Insert Format Tools Table

Break...
Page Numbers...
Date and Time...
AutoText ▶
Field...

2 Choose the AutoText command from the Insert menu.

New... Alt+F3

3 Click on New.

Create AutoText ? X

Word will create an AutoText entry from the current selection.

Please name your AutoText entry:

John Brown

OK   Cancel

4 Word suggests a name. We'll give a shorter one.

5 Enter 'sdr' and click OK.

Inserting an AutoText entry

You have now stored away an AutoText entry. John Brown's complete address is saved under the name 'sdr'. Now type 'sdr' and press the ⬚F3⬚ key. Word will insert the entire text (including the selected blank lines).

1 Type 'sdr'.

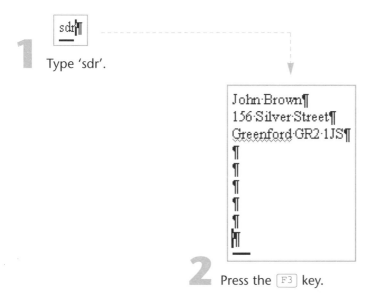

2 Press the ⬚F3⬚ key.

197

Storing more than one AutoText entry

We will now store further blocks of text in the same way.

1 Re: Your job advertisement in the

Store this under the name 'ReJob'.

2 I read your job advertisement with great interest.

Give this the name 'Text1'.

3 The tasks that you describe sound very interesting and I am looking for a new challenge in my career.

Save this as 'Text2'.

4 I have been working as a production engineer for two years. During this time I have added to my knowledge by taking an Open University course.

Store this text as 'Text3'.

5 I would be very pleased to support my application by attending an interview.

This passage of text will be stored as 'Text4'.

AutoCorrect

It is best to store standard phrases or abbreviations using the AutoCorrect facility.

Take an example from real life. Suppose you take the 'Commercial Times'. You find a job advertised in it that sounds suitable and refer to the newspaper in your letter. Enter the abbreviation CT for Commercial Times in the AutoCorrect dialog box. It does not matter whether you have already typed in and selected the text, or whether you enter it directly into the dialog box.

1 Type 'Commercial Times'.

| Commercial Times |

2 Select the text.

| Commercial Times |

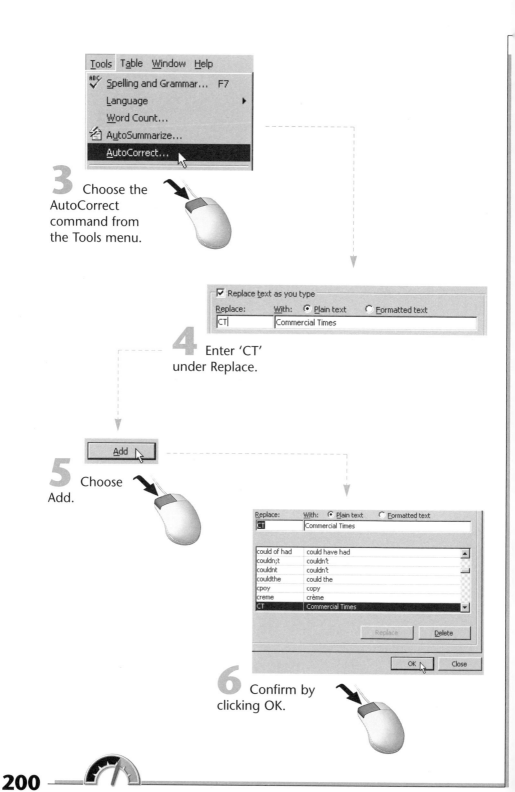

3 Choose the AutoCorrect command from the Tools menu.

4 Enter 'CT' under Replace.

5 Choose Add.

6 Confirm by clicking OK.

Still more abbreviations...

We'll store a few more abbreviations in the AutoCorrect facility as there are other newspapers that John Brown reads. These are the 'Greenford Guardian' and 'Engineering Weekly'.

It does not matter whether you use lower or upper case when entering an AutoText name.

We will also enter recurring standard phrases such as 'Dear Sirs' and 'Yours faithfully'. Save the following standard phrases in the AutoCorrect facility as you have already learnt to do.

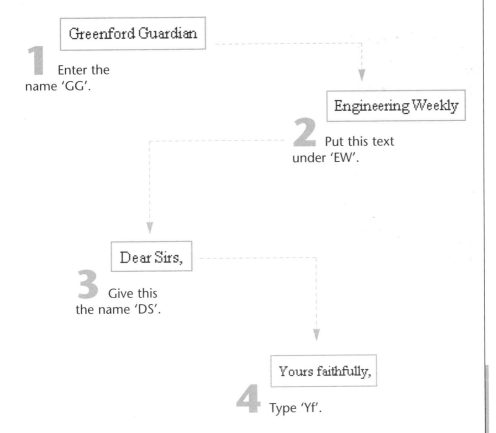

Greenford Guardian

1 Enter the name 'GG'.

Engineering Weekly

2 Put this text under 'EW'.

Dear Sirs,

3 Give this the name 'DS'.

Yours faithfully,

4 Type 'Yf'.

Using AutoText entries, AutoCorrect and tips in a letter

A quick letter

Now that we've set up our tips, AutoTexts and AutoCorrect entries, we can compose a letter using them. You'll be surprised how quickly this can be done when everything has been saved away 'in advance'. Let's have a go!

Open a new document, and you're ready to start the letter. First type in 'sdr' and press the F3 key. Word automatically inserts John Brown's name and address together with the blank lines.

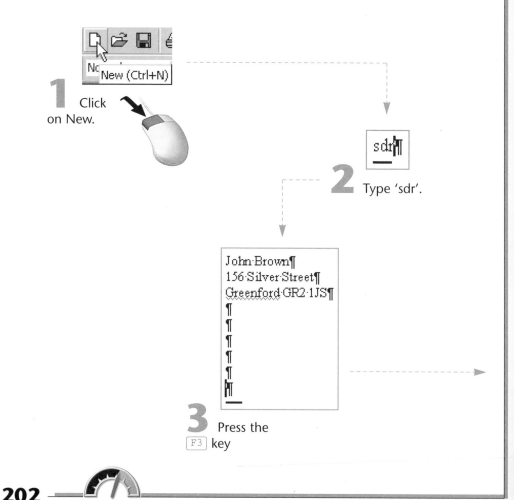

1 Click on New.

2 Type 'sdr'.

John·Brown¶
156·Silver·Street¶
Greenford·GR2·1JS¶

3 Press the F3 key

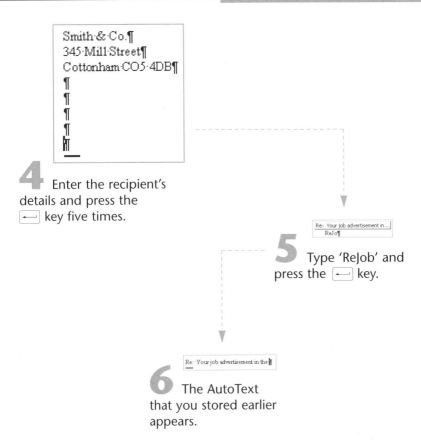

Smith & Co.¶
345 Mill Street¶
Cottonham CO5 4DB¶
¶
¶
¶
¶
¶

4 Enter the recipient's details and press the ⏎ key five times.

Re: Your job advertisement in...
ReJo¶

5 Type 'ReJob' and press the ⏎ key.

Re: Your job advertisement in the ¶

6 The AutoText that you stored earlier appears.

Where did you see it?

You saw the advert in the 'Commercial Times'. This is entered in AutoCorrect under the abbreviation 'CT'. All you need to do now is type in 'CT', press the ⎵ Space bar, and Word will automatically insert the full name of the paper.

Re: Your job advertisement in the CT¶

1 Type 'CT'.

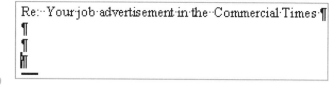

2 Press the Space bar.

Re:·Your·job·advertisement·in·the··Commercial·Times·¶
¶
¶
¶

3 Press the ← key three times.

The salutation

Now follows the salutation 'Dear Sirs,' that you have stored under 'DS'.

1 Type DS.

2 Press the Space bar.

The text

Next come a number of blocks of text. Type in their names and press the F3 key.

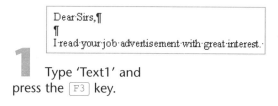

Dear·Sirs,¶
¶
I·read·your·job·advertisement·with·great·interest.·

1 Type 'Text1' and press the F3 key.

Dear Sirs,¶
¶
I read your job advertisement with great interest. The tasks that you describe sound very interesting and I am looking for a new challenge in my career. ¶
¶

2 Type 'Text2', and press the F3 key.

Dear Sirs,¶
¶
I read your job advertisement with great interest. The tasks that you describe sound very interesting and I am looking for a new challenge in my career. ¶
¶
I have been working as a production engineer for two years. During this time I have added to my knowledge by taking an Open University course. ¶
¶

3 Type 'Text3' and press the F3 key.

Dear Sirs,¶
¶
I read your job advertisement with great interest. The tasks that you describe sound very interesting and I am looking for a new challenge in my career. ¶
¶
I have been working as a production engineer for two years. During this time I have added to my knowledge by taking an Open University course. ¶
¶
I would be very pleased to support my application by attending an interview. ¶
¶
¶

4 Type 'Text4' and press the F3 key.

Closing

Generally you choose from a variety of set phrases to close a letter. Here we simply type 'Yf' and press the Space bar. This becomes 'Yours faithfully,'.

205

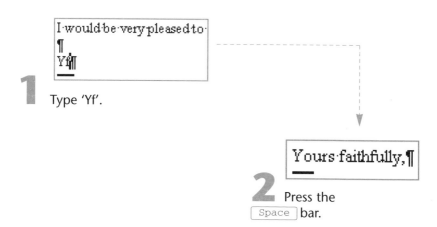

1 Type 'Yf'.

2 Press the Space bar.

Repeating the name

After the closing comes John Brown's signature, followed by his name typed in full. This means that we must add some blank lines, then repeat the name.

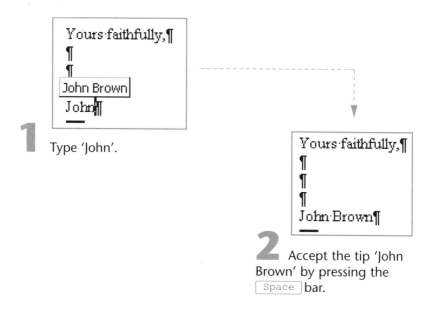

1 Type 'John'.

2 Accept the tip 'John Brown' by pressing the Space bar.

The Word Trainer

Store the following AutoText entries:

Text	AutoText Name
Engineering Works 111 Canal Street Ironford IA7 5PS	sdr
Re: Your job application dated Re: Your telephone enquiry of	re1 re2
Dear Mr Dear Mrs Dear Miss Dear Ms	sal1 sal2 sal3 sal4
Thank you for your interest in our company Please send us your Curriculum Vitae and details of two referees You are invited to an interview on Unfortunately, on this occasion your application has not been successful We wish you all the best in your future career	tex1 tex2 tex3 tex4 tex5
Yours sincerely,	cls

Compose letters to the three people below using the AutoText entries you have stored. Add the missing details.

1. Peter Jones, 96 High Street, Newtown NT2 1QJ re2 02.02, sal1, tex1, tex2, cls
2. Rosemary Sanders, 56 Coleridge Way, Walton WA7 9KM, re1 01.02, sal3, tex1, tex3 17.03, cls
3. Jane Black, 299 Lupin Drive, Woodbury IP6 9RS, re1 03.02, sal4, tex1, tex4, tex5, cls

207

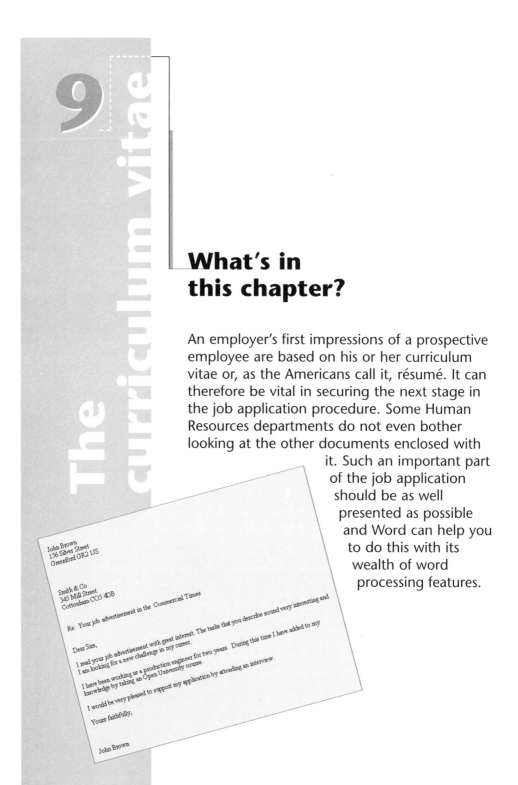

9

The curriculum vitae

What's in
this chapter?

An employer's first impressions of a prospective
employee are based on his or her curriculum
vitae or, as the Americans call it, résumé. It can
therefore be vital in securing the next stage in
the job application procedure. Some Human
Resources departments do not even bother
looking at the other documents enclosed with
it. Such an important part
of the job application
should be as well
presented as possible
and Word can help you
to do this with its
wealth of word
processing features.

John Brown
156 Silver Street
Greenford GR2 1JS

Smith & Co.
345 Mill Street
Cottonham CO5 4DB

Re: Your job advertisement in the Commercial Times

Dear Sirs,

I read your job advertisement with great interest. The tasks that you describe sound very interesting and
I am looking for a new challenge in my career.

I have been working as a production engineer for two years. During this time I have added to my
knowledge by taking an Open University course.

I would be very pleased to support my application by attending an interview.

Yours faithfully,

John Brown

Preparing your curriculum vitae yourself

You can draw up a CV using what you already know (tabs). To do this, you open a new document, give it the heading 'Curriculum Vitae' and emphasise it using the various formats (font, font size, bold, italic and underline). Then you leave a few blank lines between the heading and the information. Next you write 'Personal Information' such as 'Name, Nationality, Date of birth, Place of birth, Marital status'. You enter your details in a column on the right of your document. Use the left tab so that the information is neatly aligned.

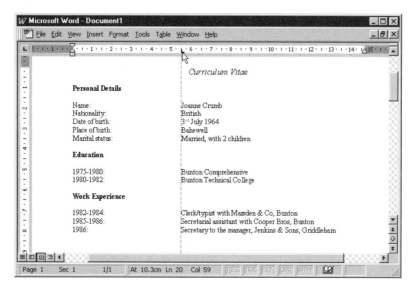

Continue the CV with 'Work experience/Professional career, Qualifications, Hobbies'.

Then save your CV. If anything in your life changes, you can enter this and save it again. In this way, you can react quickly to a job advertisement, you have your application ready and are one up on the competition.

Word's templates

WHAT'S THIS?

Document templates are models for designing documents.

You already know how to create a new document. There are two ways. One is via the New button in the Standard toolbar. Word immediately opens a new document on the screen. The other is via the New command on the File menu. When you choose New, a dialog box appears. Click on one of the tabs and you'll see a selection of templates or ready prepared documents.

WHAT'S THIS?

Templates are models for creating documents.

Templates contain suggestions that you can use. You can often tell from their names what will be

Contemporary Resume   Elegant Resume   Professional Resume

in them. Word offers you a selection of Résumés, or curricula vitae. You'll find these on the Other Documents page. You can make use of the suggestions, change them and enter your personal details.

Max Benson

Objective	[Click here and type objective]		
Experience	1990–1994	Arbor Shoe	Southridge, SC
	National Sales Manager		
	▪ Increased sales from $50 million to $100 million.		
	▪ Doubled sales per representative from $5 million to $10 million.		
	▪ Suggested new products that increased earnings by 23%.		
	1985–1990	Ferguson and Bardell	Southridge, SC
	District Sales Manager		
	▪ Increased regional sales from $25 million to $350 million.		
	▪ Managed 250 sales representatives in 10 Western states.		
	▪ Implemented training course for new recruits —speeding profitability.		
	1980–1984	Duffy Vineyards	Southridge, SC

Select one of these templates and click OK. You can also double-click the template you want. Either way will achieve the desired result of opening the template. This time you get a ready prepared text instead of the usual empty document. In fact it is not a document, but a template, and you can simply overwrite the suggestions with your data.

TIP

A document name always ends with the suffix '.DOC', while a template name ends with '.DOT'.

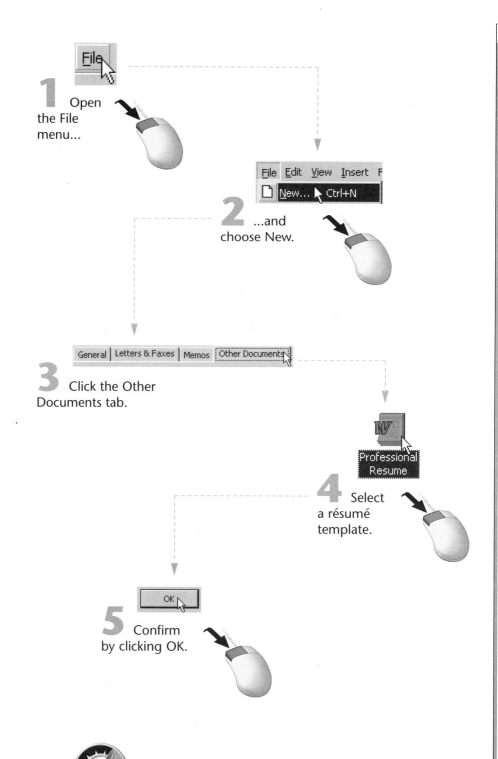

1 Open the File menu...

File Edit View Insert F

New... Ctrl+N

2 ...and choose New.

General | Letters & Faxes | Memos | Other Documents

3 Click the Other Documents tab.

Professional Resume

4 Select a résumé template.

OK

5 Confirm by clicking OK.

The CV Wizard

In addition to the templates, Word also provides you with Wizards. These can take some of the some of the work off your hands. For example, Word offers you help with letters and faxes (on the Letters & Faxes page). You can also get help with your CV from the Other Documents page where you will find the CV Wizard.

Resume Wizard

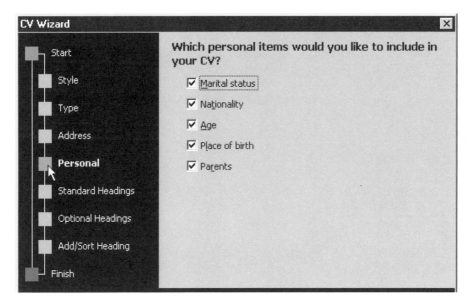

A wizard takes you step by step to your goal. Start it by double-clicking its icon, and you'll see a rather strange-looking dialog box. Don't be fazed! It's really easy.

In the left-hand column, the box next to 'Start' is coloured green. You can tell from these boxes what stage you have reached in the Wizard. They also show you which stage you are currently working on. If you click another selection, you skip over the other stages. In the right-hand column you decide what information you are going to give. This is generally done just by clicking with the mouse. Click on the Next button at the bottom of the dialog box to move on to the next point.

213

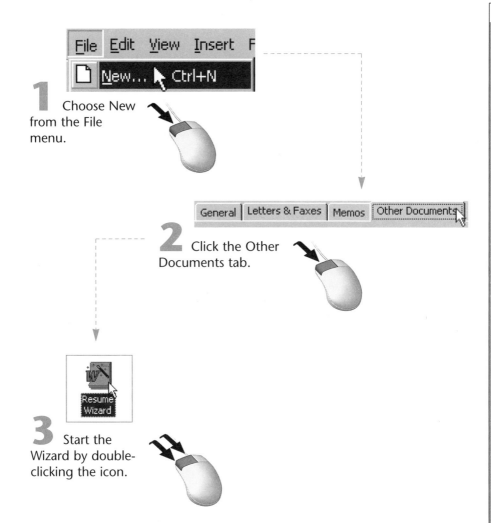

1 Choose New from the File menu.

2 Click the Other Documents tab.

3 Start the Wizard by double-clicking the icon.

The CV Wizard is now open on your screen and you can proceed a step at a time. Click the Next button to move on.

The first window you see is purely informative. Click the Next button.

First you need to choose the style of your CV. Decide on one of the versions offered. For this exercise choose Contemporary. If you don't like this style you can change it later on.

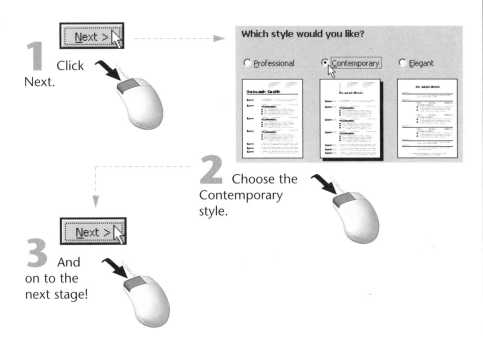

1 Click Next.

2 Choose the Contemporary style.

3 And on to the next stage!

Now you need to choose the type of CV. For example, you could pick 'Entry-level CV' or 'Professional CV'. Most users find that the 'Chronological CV' is appropriate, so choose this one.

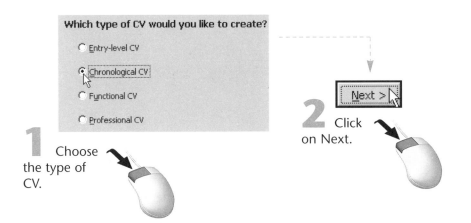

1 Choose the type of CV.

2 Click on Next.

215

Enter your address in the next text box. There is no need to give your email address, so leave that field out. If you don't fill in a field it will be ignored later.

What is your name and mailing address?

Name:	Joanne Crumb
Address:	37 Church Lane Great Norton Staffs. GN4 8MA
Phone:	
Fax:	
Email:	

1 Fill in your data.

Next >

2 What do we go next?

In the next text box you choose the entries for your CV. Indicate that you want Marital status, Nationality, etc., but you don't have to give details about your parents!

Next comes information that describes your qualifications, such as professional experience, training etc. Click the entries you want and leave the others – they will not then be listed later.

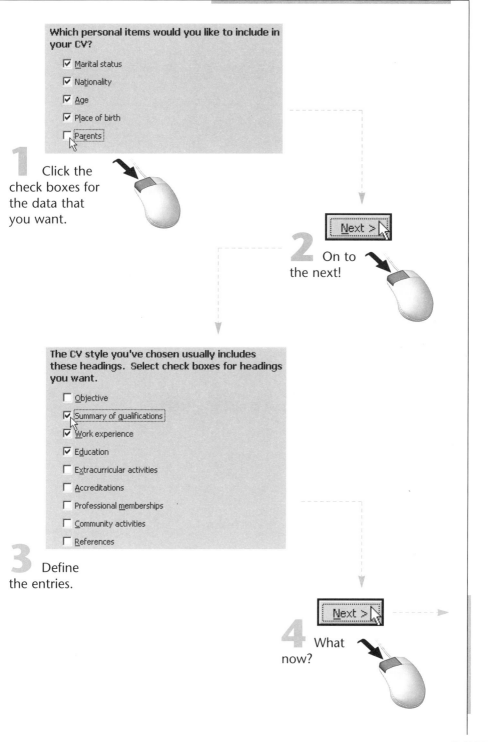

Which personal items would you like to include in your CV?

☑ Marital status
☑ Nationality
☑ Age
☑ Place of birth
☐ Parents

1 Click the check boxes for the data that you want.

Next >

2 On to the next!

The CV style you've chosen usually includes these headings. Select check boxes for headings you want.

☐ Objective
☑ Summary of qualifications
☑ Work experience
☑ Education
☐ Extracurricular activities
☐ Accreditations
☐ Professional memberships
☐ Community activities
☐ References

3 Define the entries.

Next >

4 What now?

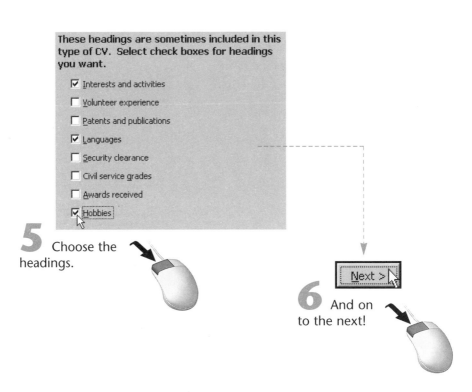

These headings are sometimes included in this type of CV. Select check boxes for headings you want.

☑ Interests and activities
☐ Volunteer experience
☐ Patents and publications
☑ Languages
☐ Security clearance
☐ Civil service grades
☐ Awards received
☑ Hobbies

5 Choose the headings.

6 And on to the next!

Next >

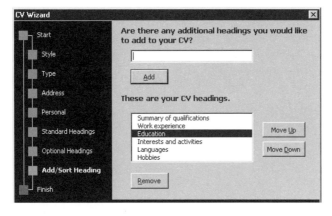

CV Wizard

Start
Style
Type
Address
Personal
Standard Headings
Optional Headings
Add/Sort Heading
Finish

Are there any additional headings you would like to add to your CV?

Add

These are your CV headings.

Summary of qualifications
Work experience
Education
Interests and activities
Languages
Hobbies

Move Up
Move Down

Remove

On the next page you can take control of the action again. You can have another think about the headings in your CV. If you want to add to them, fill in the new ones, then click Add. If you want to delete a heading, select it and then click the Remove button. The order of the headings is especially important. You can change this using the Move Up and Move Down buttons.

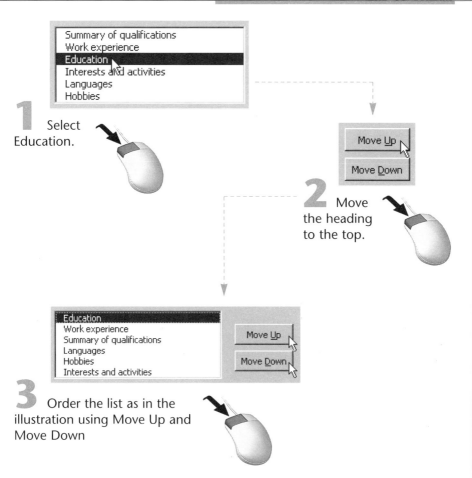

1 Select Education.

2 Move the heading to the top.

3 Order the list as in the illustration using Move Up and Move Down

You could now terminate the CV Wizard by clicking the Finish button. However, we'll do it by the book and follow every step, so click Next. Word will confirm that all the information has been entered. Now you can click Finish. A little helper – the Office Assistant – appears on the screen and offers you help on various points. You could change the style of your CV here if you wish. However, all is as it should be and you can click Cancel. The Office Assistant disappears from the screen. Now you can view the finished template on screen. All you need do next is fill in your personal data.

219

1 Click Next for the last time.

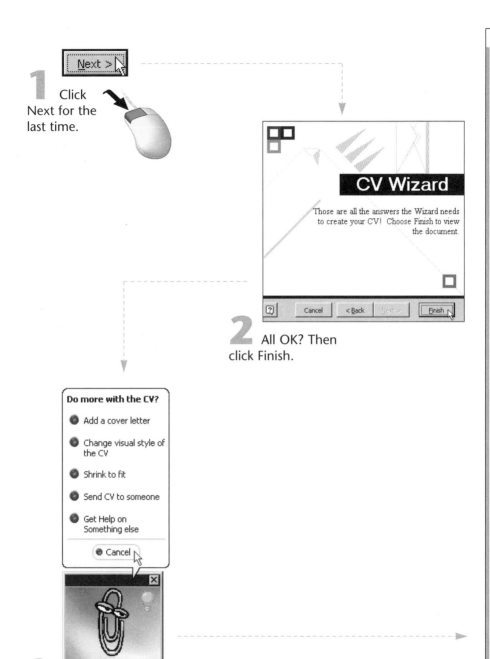

CV Wizard

Those are all the answers the Wizard needs to create your CV! Choose Finish to view the document.

Cancel | < Back | Next > | Finish

2 All OK? Then click Finish.

Do more with the CV?

● Add a cover letter

● Change visual style of the CV

● Shrink to fit

● Send CV to someone

● Get Help on Something else

● Cancel

3 Make our little helper disappear by clicking Cancel.

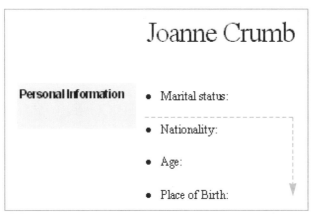

4 The template appears on your screen and all you
need do is fill in your details.

The Word Trainer

Word does not only have a store of templates and an assistant for
CVs. You'll find further examples in the other properties sheets.

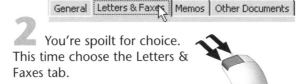

1 When you want to use
a template, it's important
that you choose New from
the File menu.

2 You're spoilt for choice.
This time choose the Letters &
Faxes tab.

221

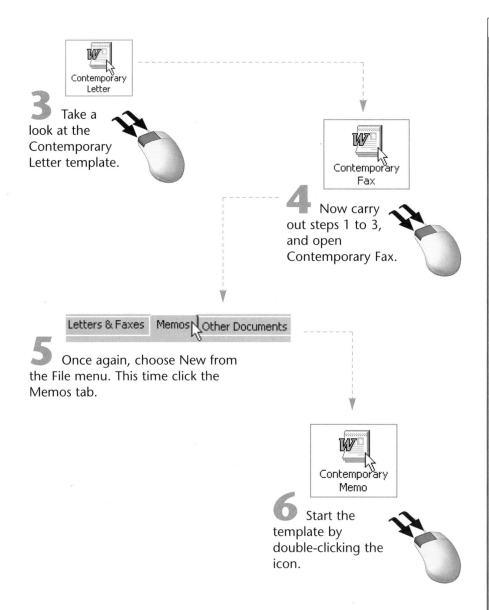

3 Take a look at the Contemporary Letter template.

4 Now carry out steps 1 to 3, and open Contemporary Fax.

Letters & Faxes   Memos   Other Documents

5 Once again, choose New from the File menu. This time click the Memos tab.

6 Start the template by double-clicking the icon.

In Word you'll find a whole range of Wizards. They are largely identical to the CV Wizard in their appearance and how you use them.

1 Start the Memo Wizard (choose New from the File menu, then click the Memos tab).

2 Choose New from the File menu again, and now click the Letters & Faxes tab.

3 Take a look at the Letter Wizard.

Writing a letter of complaint

What's in this chapter?

Mr Grump is beside himself with rage! He has just come back from a holiday that was a disaster from start to finish. He reckons he didn't deserve such a catalogue of woes. Scarcely has he set foot inside the front door when he sits down in front of his computer, still seething. To emphasise the things that went wrong, he gives each a number. When he has calmed down a bit, he goes back to correct his letter. He turns sentences round and replaces frequently used words.

Dear Mr Steele,

I rented your house on the island of Tobaluba from 17.05 to 27.05. It could scarcely be called a relaxing holiday. The dwelling did not come up to my expectations; there were a number of shortcomings. Here is a list of the deficiencies:

1. The **toilets** were constantly blocking.
2. In the **kitchen** there were no cooking utensils.
3. The cleaner only came once every 3 days.
4. The **water** in the pool was always much too cold.

In anticipation of your early reply,

Yours sincerely,

Jack Grump

You already know:

You are going to learn:

Lists with numbered points

When reading, your eye is drawn first to lists with numbered points. The most familiar type is '1,2,3,...' and, as chance would have it, there is a button for this type of list on the Formatting toolbar. If you click on it, numbers will appear as you type. Another way of making a list stand out is by using bullets.

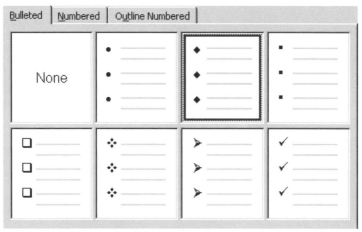

There are many types of list and they are not limited to these two buttons. Open the Format menu and choose Bullets and Numbering. Click the Bulleted tab and you will see some other ways of setting out lists.

Creating a list

If you have already written your text, select it before creating your list. However, you can also create a list first and then write the text. Word numbers it automatically when you press the ⟵ key. The list ends automatically when you leave a blank line.

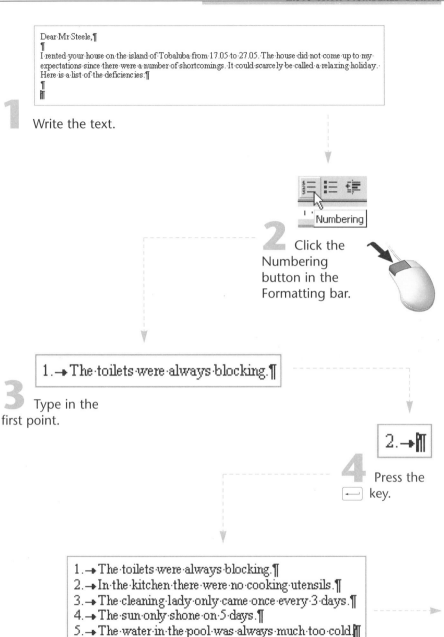

Dear·Mr·Steele,¶
¶
I·rented·your·house·on·the·island·of·Tobaluba·from·17.05·to·27.05.·The·house·did·not·come·up·to·my·
expectations·since·there·were·a·number·of·shortcomings.·It·could·scarcely·be·called·a·relaxing·holiday.·
Here·is·a·list·of·the·deficiencies:¶
¶
¶

1 Write the text.

Numbering

2 Click the Numbering button in the Formatting bar.

1.→ The·toilets·were·always·blocking.¶

3 Type in the first point.

2.→

4 Press the ⏎ key.

1.→ The·toilets·were·always·blocking.¶
2.→ In·the·kitchen·there·were·no·cooking·utensils.¶
3.→ The·cleaning·lady·only·came·once·every·3·days.¶
4.→ The·sun·only·shone·on·5·days.¶
5.→ The·water·in·the·pool·was·always·much·too·cold.¶

5 Type in the following points exactly as above. At the end of each point, press the ⏎ key.

227

```
5.→ The·water·in·the·pool·was·always·much·too·cold.¶
6.→¶
```

6 When you have entered all your points and are at the end of your list, press the ⎯ key.

```
5.→ The·water·in·the·pool·was·always·much·too·cold.¶
   ¶
   ¶
```

7 Leave the numbered point blank and press the ⎯ key again.

```
5.→ The·water·in·the·pool·was·always·much·too·cold.¶
   ¶
In·anticipation·of·your·early·reply,¶
   ¶
Yours·sincerely,¶
   ¶
   ¶
Jack·Grump¶
```

8 Now carry on with the 'normal' text.

Deleting from a list

You can also delete from a list (as here in the 'dog, cat, mouse' example). It is important that the entire line is selected. Put the mouse pointer in front of the entry to be deleted (here it is '2. Cat').

```
1.  Dog
2.  Cat
3.  Mouse
```

Select it and press the ⎀Delete⎁ key. The cat vanishes. Word automatically readjusts the numbering. The mouse, which was number 3 before, is now number 2.

```
1.  Dog
2.  Mouse
```

In our example Mr Grump also wants to delete an entry. After discussing it with his wife, he sees that he cannot complain about the lack of sunshine. So he deletes number 4.

1. → The toilets were always blocking. ¶
2. → In the kitchen there were no cooking utensils. ¶
3. → The cleaning lady only came once every 3 days. ¶
4. → The sun only shone on 5 days. ¶
5. → The water in the pool was always much too cold. ¶

1 Position the mouse pointer.

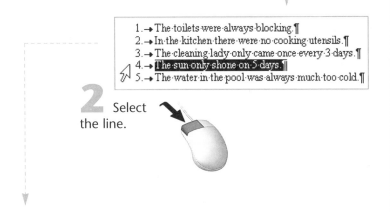

1. → The toilets were always blocking. ¶
2. → In the kitchen there were no cooking utensils. ¶
3. → The cleaning lady only came once every 3 days. ¶
4. → The sun only shone on 5 days. ¶
5. → The water in the pool was always much too cold. ¶

2 Select the line.

1. → The toilets were always blocking. ¶
2. → In the kitchen there were no cooking utensils. ¶
3. → The cleaning lady only came once every 3 days. ¶
4. → The water in the pool was always much too cold. ¶

3 Delete the point by pressing the [Delete] key.

Cutting, pasting and copying text

Cutting and pasting is about moving text that you've already typed to another place. You know the basics already: first you select the text that you want to move, then various options are open to you for the next stage.

I·rented·your·house·on·the·island·of·Tobaluba·from·17.05·to·27.05.·The·house·did·not·come·up·to·my· expectations·since·there·were·a·number·of·shortcomings.·It·could·scarcely·be·called·a·relaxing·holiday. Here·is·a·list·of·the·house's·shortcomings:

Cutting and copying using buttons

You can find the commands that we now need in the Edit menu. They can also be carried out using shortcut keys. Many books list these. But why bother with them? After all, you've got the buttons on the Standard toolbar. But, in case you're interested, you'll find a list of shortcut keys in the appendix to this book.

If you want to move a selected piece of text, click on the scissors button. This cuts out the selected text. However, if you want to duplicate the text, simply copy it by clicking on the pages button to the right of the scissors. So, selected text disappears with the scissors, but the original remains intact if you simply copy it. No matter which method you choose – and which button – what you do next is the same. Your text is now in the clipboard.

The clipboard is the short-term memory. It remains intact until you cut or copy a new text. If you shut down your computer, the data is lost. Your PC isn't suffering from loss of memory! Only saved data can be called up again after restarting the computer.

...and pasting

Next you have to move the cursor to the place where the block of text is to be inserted. Then simply click the Insert button. You can keep on taking the same text from the clipboard until you cut or copy something new.

Cutting and copying with the mouse

Drag and drop means moving the cursor to, for example, a file icon, pressing and holding down the left mouse button while moving the file icon to a new location, then letting it go by releasing the mouse button.

Now it's the mouse's turn! For seasoned mouse users, this method is even quicker. It's called drag and drop.

To drag and drop a block of text, you pick it up, move it and drop it into position like this. Place the mouse pointer just in front of the selected text and hold down the left mouse button. A dotted rectangle appears under the mouse pointer, which is Word's way of indicating that you can now move the selection. A dotted line appears in front of the mouse pointer. Keep holding down the mouse button and move the dotted line to where you would like to insert the text. Then release

If things go wrong when you cut and paste or drag and drop, and the text ends up in the wrong place, simply click the Undo button. This undoes the last command. Your screen will then look exactly as if nothing had happened and you can try again.

the mouse button. The text disappears from its old position and appears in the new one. By the way, you can also copy using the mouse

button. Employ the same procedure you used for moving the text, but press the `Ctrl` key as well. A plus sign (+) appears at the mouse pointer.

1 Select the text.

It could scarcely be called a relaxing holiday.

> It·could·scarcely·be·called·a·relaxing·holiday.·

2 Press the left mouse button
and hold it down, then...

> :The·house·did·not

3 ...drag
the text to
the new
position.

> I·rented·your·house·on·the·island·of·Tobaluba·from·17.05·to·27.05.·It·could·scarcely·be·called·a·
> relaxing·holiday.·The·house·did·not·come·up·to·my·expectations·since·there·were·a·number·of·

4 When you release the mouse button,
the text will have moved.

While you are doing drag and drop, you can still scroll
through a document. Drag the selected text towards the
edge of the window until the white mouse pointer changes
into a black one. Word scrolls up or down by itself.

The Thesaurus

'The house next to our house was larger than the house diagonally
opposite.' This sentence can hardly be called good English prose,
because of the repetition. House, house, house – you can't help
noticing that this word is overused. But what other word could you
use? A house is, after all, a house. If you're stuck for alternatives, use
the Thesaurus under Language on the Tools menu. This may sound
like something that has escaped from Jurassic Park, but it really can
be a very friendly beast. It's there to suggest alternative ways of
expressing similar concepts. Writers use this resource frequently –
and so does the author of this book.

WHAT'S THIS?

The Thesaurus shows you synonyms for a word, so that you can put more variety into your text. Collins English Dictionary defines a thesaurus as a 'book containing systematised lists of synonyms and related words'.

'The house next to our residence was larger than the building diagonally opposite.' This sounds a bit better than the first version and would be preferred by any English teacher.

Other examples could be: 'hamper' instead of 'basket', 'earth' instead of 'soil', 'lawn' instead of 'grass'.

I rented your house on the island of Tobaluba from 17.05 to 27.05. It could scarcely be called a relaxing holiday. The house did not come up to my expectations since there were a number of shortcomings. Here is a list of the house's shortcomings:

In our letter, Mr Grump in his over-eagerness used the same words repeatedly. There are houses all over the place. You only need to put the cursor on a word and Word knows that you are looking for another way of saying this term. Click the Tools menu and find the Thesaurus under Language. Meanings shows you the direction that the various synonyms take (in this case 'habitation', 'business', 'governing body' or 'reside' – three nouns and a verb).

TIP

To start the Thesaurus you can also press the ⎡o⎤ + ⎡F7⎤ keys.

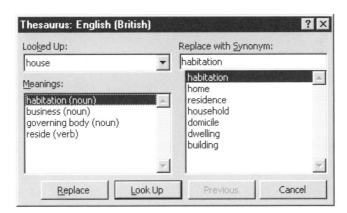

233

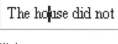

1 Click on the word.

2 Open the Thesaurus by clicking the Tools menu and choosing Language/Thesaurus.

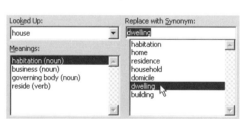

3 Choose 'dwelling'.

4 Confirm by clicking on Replace.

Since we are now familiar with the Thesaurus, we will frequently make use of it. Mr Grump has used two more identical expressions in his letter. These are 'always' and 'shortcomings'. Replace these with other words using the Thesaurus.

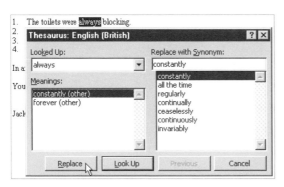

1 Replace 'always' by 'constantly'.

2 Now we want to exchange the word 'shortcomings', but there is a problem. Word knows only that this is related to the word 'shortcoming' and tells us so.

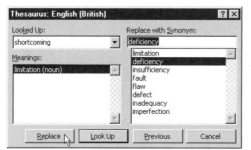

3 Click the 'Lookup' button. The thesaurus looks up the word 'shortcoming' and makes some (singular) suggestions. Choose 'deficiency' and click 'Replace'.

Here is a list of the deficiencies

4 We have to make the final change ourselves. Press the backspace key to delete the 'y' and replace it with 'ies' to create the plural word. It may not be automatic, but it's still quicker than reaching for Roget!

Find and replace

Seek and you shall find. The motto also applies to Word. How often have you used the wrong expression when writing a letter or other text? Say you were writing instructions on how to use a battery and you had got 'plus' and 'minus' muddled up – that could have fatal consequences for the reader. You can see what you're doing with a short text, but if the document has 5, 10, 50 or even more pages it's another matter. Do you really want to go through the document page by page on the screen? You may strain your eyes and yet still miss things. With Word, you can choose one of two functions to help you. Choose Find from the Edit menu and Word will just track down the word. Use the Replace command just below it if you want to replace the word by another expression. We have made it really easy in our example! Our document has been kept (extra) short so that you can make the change immediately. Mr Grump wants to replace 'cleaning lady' by 'cleaner'. Of course he can see this on the screen. However, you're now going to familiarise yourself with the Find and Replace function.

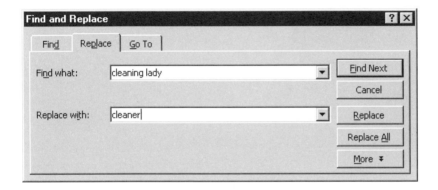

Mr Grump fills in the word he wants to look for and enters the replacement word. If you click the Replace button, Word replaces the words one at a time if there is more than one occurrence. It asks each time whether the word should be replaced. The process is faster if you use Replace All, as all instances of the search words are automatically replaced. Word finishes by telling you how many words have been found and replaced.

TIP

If you click the More button, you can specify whether upper case and lower case are important and/or whether or not the search word is a whole word.

237

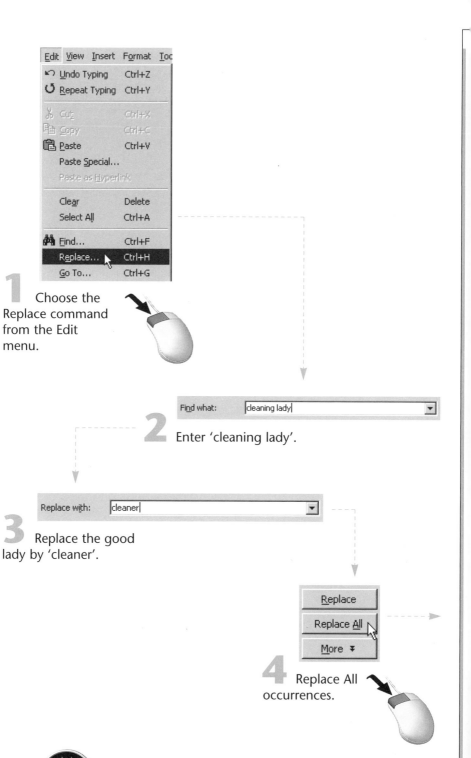

1 Choose the Replace command from the Edit menu.

Find what: | cleaning lady|

2 Enter 'cleaning lady'.

Replace with: | cleaner|

3 Replace the good lady by 'cleaner'.

Replace
Replace All
More ∓

4 Replace All occurrences.

Microsoft Word

Word has completed its search of the document and has made 1 replacement.

OK

5 Word tells you how many times the replacement has been made.

The Format Painter

Mr Grump would now like to emphasise in bold some words that appear important to him. You could do this one word at a time. However, there is a

1. The **toilets** were constantly blocking.
2. In the **kitchen** there were no cooking utensils.
3. The **cleaner** only came once every 3 days.
4. The **water** in the pool was always much too cold.

 quicker way. You must have noticed the paintbrush in the Standard toolbar, and perhaps you wondered what it is for.

Now you will find out. Using the paintbrush you can transfer formats – that's why it's called the Format Painter. For example, if a word is already in bold, click on it. Now activate the Format Painter with a click of the mouse, and your

 If you click the Format Painter button once, you can only transfer formats once. Double-click it and you can use the function as often as you like.

mouse pointer changes appearance. If you click on another word, the bold is transferred. The Format Painter switches itself off. However, if you double-click the paintbrush button, you can transfer the format repeatedly until you click the button again or press the Esc key.

The **t**oilets

1 Put the cursor on the word 'toilets'.

2 Format it in Bold.

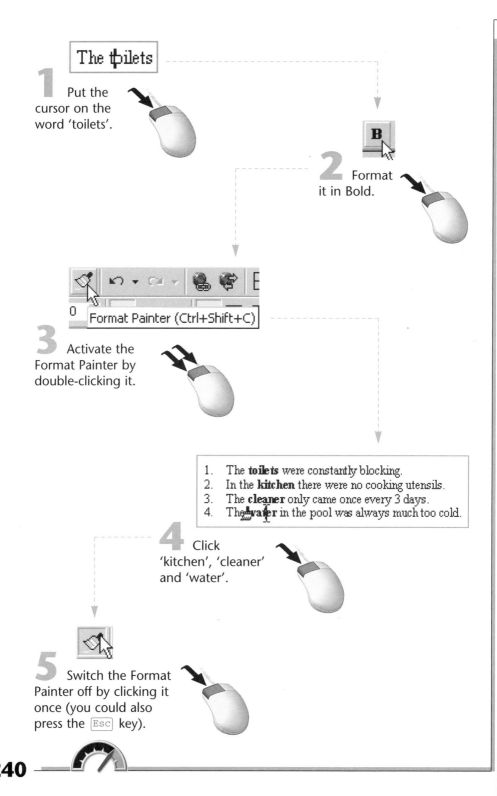

Format Painter (Ctrl+Shift+C)

3 Activate the Format Painter by double-clicking it.

1. The **toilets** were constantly blocking.
2. In the **kitchen** there were no cooking utensils.
3. The **cleaner** only came once every 3 days.
4. The **water** in the pool was always much too cold.

4 Click 'kitchen', 'cleaner' and 'water'.

5 Switch the Format Painter off by clicking it once (you could also press the Esc key).

The Word Trainer

Lists

> These are the creatures the old lady swallowed:
>
> 1. Fly
> 2. Spider
> 3. Bird
> 4. Cat
> 5. Dog
> 6. Cow
> 7. Horse

1 Copy the text and list the unfortunate creatures that were supposed to catch each other.

2 Select the creatures,...

3 ...and have fun choosing different formats using the Bulleted and Numbered properties sheets to be found under Format/Bullets and Numbering.

241

Drag and drop

> On Saturdays we drive out into the countryside. On Saturdays we have a day off. The sun usually shines on Saturdays.

1 Type in what you usually do on Saturdays.

> On Saturdays we have a day off.

2 Now move the third sentence in front of the second.

Replace

> On Saturdays we drive out into the countryside. The sun usually shines on Saturdays. On Saturdays we have a day off.

1 Who goes out for the day on Saturdays? Saturday is shopping day, and Sunday is the day for driving into the countryside. So change the days using Edit/Replace.

| Find what: | Saturday | ▾ |
| Replace with: | Sunday | ▾ |

2 Time is money! Replace all the days in one go.

3 Word reports back: Saturday was
replaced by Sunday three times,...

> On Sundays we drive out into the countryside. The sun usually shines on Sundays. On Sundays we have a day off.

4 ... so, let's go,
shall we?

Thesaurus

> Man
> Woman
> Correct
> Ship
> Murder

What's the difference between a man
and a woman? If you don't know, the
Thesaurus will tell you.

The Format Painter

> On Monday the decorators were supposed to come, but they didn't arrive. Now I'm standing here with my paint pots and brushes. What am I to do? Do it yourself, I thought. You have to get on and do things yourself. I dipped my brush into the first paint pot. After two days my flat was freshly painted from top to bottom. I looked at my handiwork, left the house and moved in with my girlfriend. Since then I have never been back to my flat.

1 Type in this story of everyday life.

243

the **dec̲o̲rators** were supposed
t pots and brushes. What am I

2 Format
decorators in bold and
underline it. Leave the
cursor on the word.

On Monday the **dec̲o̲rators** were supposed to come, but they didn't arrive. Now I'm standing here
with my **paint pots** and brushes. What am I to do? Do it yourself, I thought. You have to get on and
do things yourself. I dipped my brush into the first paint pot. After two days my **flat** was freshly
painted from top to bottom. I looked at my handiwork, left the house and moved in with my
girlfriend. Since then I have never been back to my flat.

3 Transfer the format
using the Format Painter.

come, but they didn't arrive. N
o do? *Do it yourself* I thought.
e first paint pot. After two days

4 Format these
words in italic.

On Monday the **dec̲o̲rators** were supposed to come, but they didn't arrive. Now I'm standing here
with my **paint pots** and brushes. What am I to do? *Do it yourself,* I thought. *You have to get on and
do things yourself.* I dipped my brush into the first paint pot. After two days my **flat** was freshly
painted from top to bottom. I looked at my handiwork, left the house and moved in with my
girlfriend. Since then I have never been back to my flat.

5 Paint other words
with this format.

What's in this chapter?

On occasions such as Christmas, Easter and birthdays it's traditional to send greetings cards. They are especially welcome if they have been created personally by hand. Word enables you to send greetings with a personal touch by allowing you to adapt designs to your individual taste. There are no limits to the imagination. You can insert names and special features and – if you like doing that sort of thing – turn the Easter Bunny on his head and make him feel dizzy.

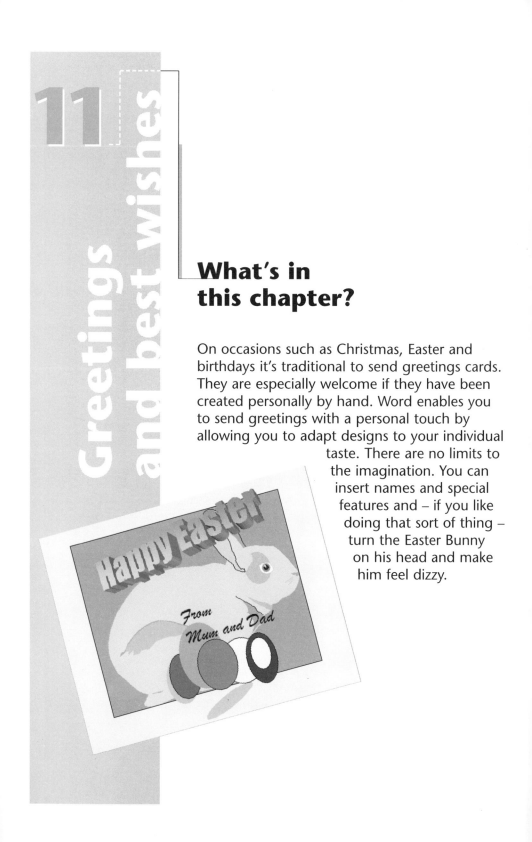

You already know:

You are going to learn:

247

Inserting a Clip Art graphic

Word offers you the chance to be artistic. With the help of the Drawing toolbar and a little practice, you can create the most wonderful paintings. However, if you're a bit short on artistic talent, Word can offer you ready-to-use pictures. These are called Clip Art, and you can find them by clicking the Insert menu and choosing Picture then Clip Art.

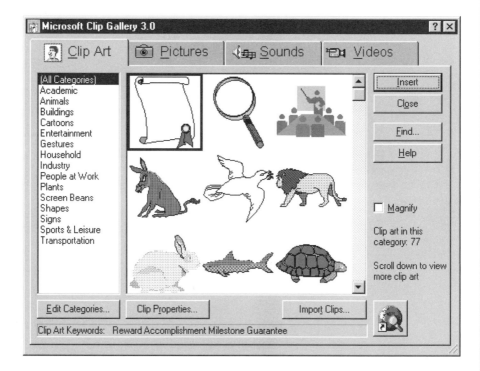

If you click
the Magnify ☑ Magnify
check box,
the pictures are easier
to see.

In the Clip Art properties sheet you'll find a number of categories. The pictures are grouped under various headings such as Household, Cartoons and Animals. If you select (All Categories) you can view all the Clip Art images. Use the scroll bar to view all the pictures.

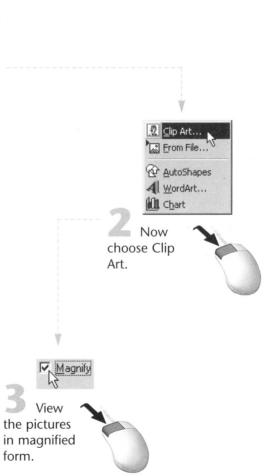

1 Click the Insert menu and choose Picture.

2 Now choose Clip Art.

3 View the pictures in magnified form.

Picking out a Clip Art

You can either select a picture by clicking on it with the mouse or by using the cursor keys. Insert a picture using the Insert button. However, there is an even quicker way. Double-click on the picture and Word inserts it in the document.

In our example we'll take the Easter Bunny for an Easter card (or is it a hare?). Each picture has a title.

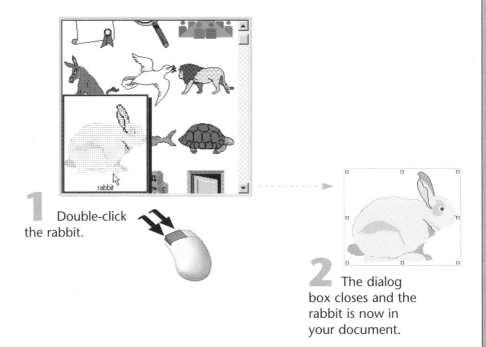

1 Double-click the rabbit.

2 The dialog box closes and the rabbit is now in your document.

Editing a graphic

Before you can edit a graphic you must click on it.

Around the rabbit you will see small squares, or sizing handles. These mark the limit of our Clip Art graphic. You can get rid of the sizing handles by clicking outside the picture. However, if you want to edit a graphic, they must be activated. Click on the rabbit and the sizing handles will reappear around it.

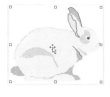

If you point to the middle of the selected graphic, the mouse pointer appears as a kind of cross-hairs. If this is visible, you can move the graphic around in your document by holding down the left mouse button and dragging it. Position the mouse pointer on one of the square dots, and you can change the size of the graphic as indicated by the direction of the arrow.

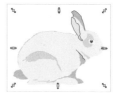

If the rabbit appears a little too large on your monitor and you cannot see all of it properly, simply reduce the Zoom factor. You don't have to do this – it's only a suggestion since the Zoom function has no effect on how the document looks when you print it.

90% ▼
500%
200%
150%
100%
75%
50%
25%
10%
Page Width
Whole Page
Two Pages

1 If you want to, change the Zoom factor.

251

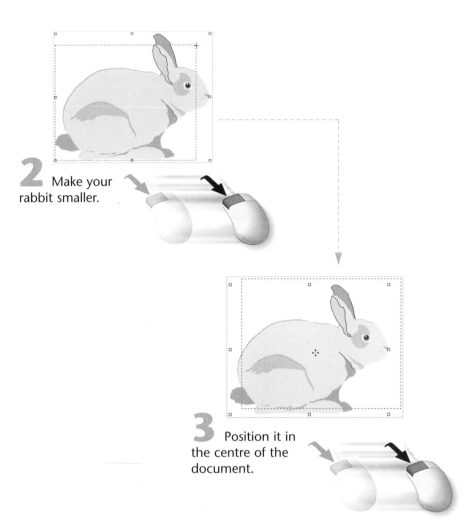

2 Make your rabbit smaller.

3 Position it in the centre of the document.

The Drawing toolbar

The Drawing toolbar must be called up specially. To do this, click the Draw icon. As soon as this happens, the Drawing toolbar appears, usually at the bottom of the screen. Here you'll see all sorts of functions that we'll go into in more detail in this and the following chapters.

What's the background going to be?

For this we need the button with the tipping paint pot. Use it to determine the Fill Color of an area. If you don't want the area to be filled with colour, click No Fill.

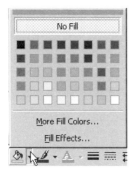

If you click the small triangle next to the paint pot, you are given a choice of colours. Now click the graphic and choose a background colour. What would suit a rabbit better than green?

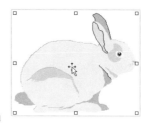

1 Click the Drawing toolbar button on the Standard toolbar.

2 Click the triangle next to the Fill Color button.

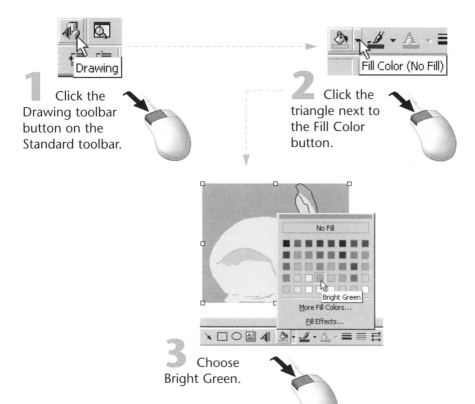

3 Choose Bright Green.

253

Line Color

You can frame the picture with a line. As with the Fill Color, you have a choice of lots of different colours. For this you need the button on the Drawing toolbar that shows a paintbrush (Line Color). Click on the small triangle and choose your colour. Here we'll use black. If you choose No Line, the border disappears.

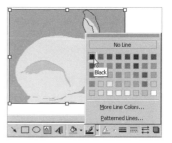

1 Click the triangle next to Line Color.

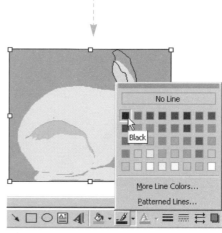

2 Choose the colour Black.

Shapes

Using the buttons on the Drawing toolbar, you can draw shapes such as rectangles or circles. How about giving the Easter Bunny some eggs? The ellipse is best for this. Click on the Ellipse button and adjust the size and shape of the egg using the mouse button. At Easter we have colourful Easter Eggs. This is not a problem – use the Fill Color button to add some colour.

1 Click the Ellipse button on the Drawing toolbar.

2 Position the mouse pointer on the graphic.

3 Drag the mouse to adjust the shape.

Fill Color (No Fill)

4 Click on the Fill Color small triangle.

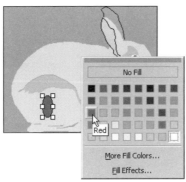

5 Chose a bright colour.

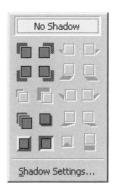

6 Make some more Easter Eggs using steps 1 to 5.

Shadows

On the Drawing toolbar you'll find the Shadow button. You can use this to put a shadow behind a graphic. This does not have to be our Easter Eggs, but could also be a Clip Art graphic. You can throw the shadow from above, below, left or right. There are quite a number of optical effects for you to choose from.

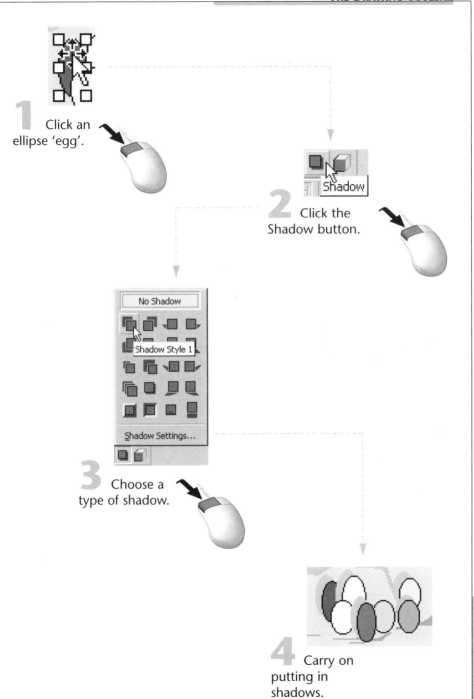

Click an
ellipse 'egg'.

Shadow

Click the
Shadow button.

No Shadow

Shadow Style 1

Shadow Settings...

Choose a
type of shadow.

Carry on
putting in
shadows.

257

WordArt – font effects

We would like to wish someone a 'Happy Easter'. Alternatively, this could be 'Happy Birthday' or 'Best Wishes'. You can design your own lettering in an original way using WordArt. Open the application by choosing Picture/Wordart from the Insert menu or by clicking the 'A' button on the Drawing toolbar. Now indicate which effect you want by either a double-click or a single click followed by OK. A second dialog box appears in which you can set the font and font size and then enter the text.

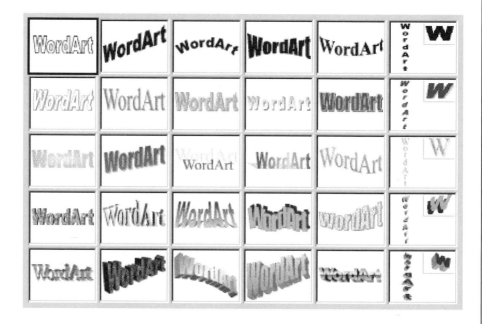

1 Click on the Insert WordArt button on the Drawing toolbar.

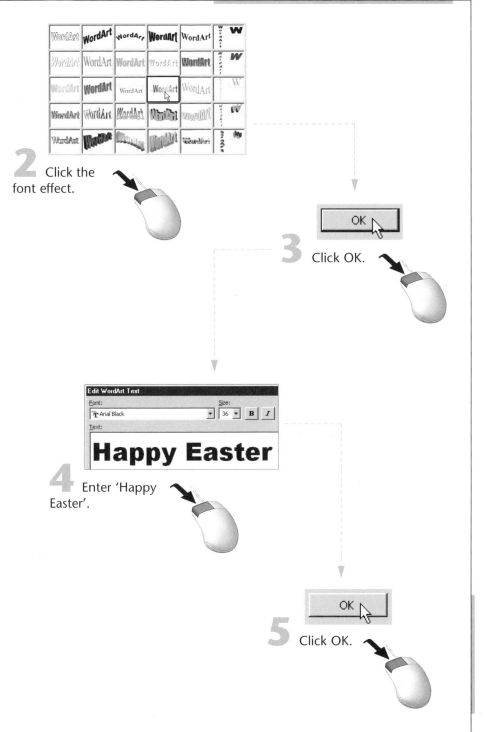

2 Click the font effect.

3 Click OK.

OK

Edit WordArt Text

Font: Arial Black | Size: 36 | **B** | *I*

Text:

Happy Easter

4 Enter 'Happy Easter'.

5 Click OK.

OK

259

Moving graphics

Your lettering – the WordArt – has been inserted. You can edit it like a normal graphic. Click on it, and around its edges the small squares will appear that you can use to change its size. If you position the mouse pointer in the middle of the lettering, the pointer changes to a 'cross-hairs'. Now you can move the lettering about.

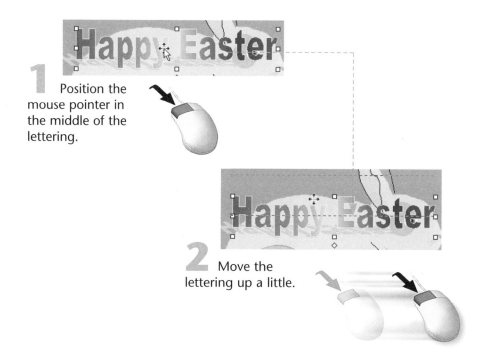

1 Position the mouse pointer in the middle of the lettering.

2 Move the lettering up a little.

Sloping lettering

Below your lettering you may have noticed a little yellow rhombus. Point the mouse at this and you can change the angle of your lettering. Drag the

rhombus to the left and the lettering will lean backwards, drag it to the right and the lettering will lean forwards. The leaning

tower of Pisa could do with something like this!

1 Move the mouse pointer up to the rhombus until the pointer changes shape.

2 Drag a little to the right.

Head first

In Word, you can turn the world on its head, for the program allows you to rotate graphics through up to 360 degrees. The button for this is found on the Drawing toolbar.

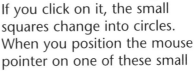

If you click on it, the small squares change into circles. When you position the mouse pointer on one of these small

circles it turns into a pivotal point. Continue to hold down the mouse button and

you can rotate the lettering however you like.

261

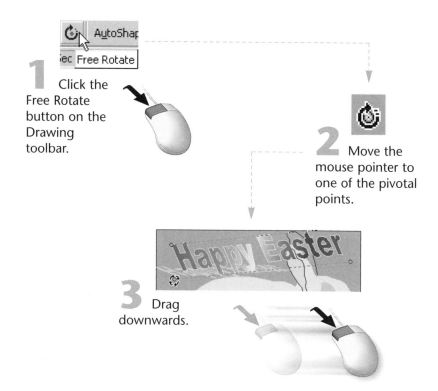

1 Click the Free Rotate button on the Drawing toolbar.

2 Move the mouse pointer to one of the pivotal points.

3 Drag downwards.

Text in pictures

You can also type ordinary text into the Easter Bunny graphic. We'll now add 'from Mum and Dad'. To do this, we need to create a text box in the graphic.

 Click the button on the Drawing toolbar to insert a text box. Then click on the graphic and drag until the box is the size you want. As you already know, you can adjust the size of the selection rectangle using the sizing handles (small squares).

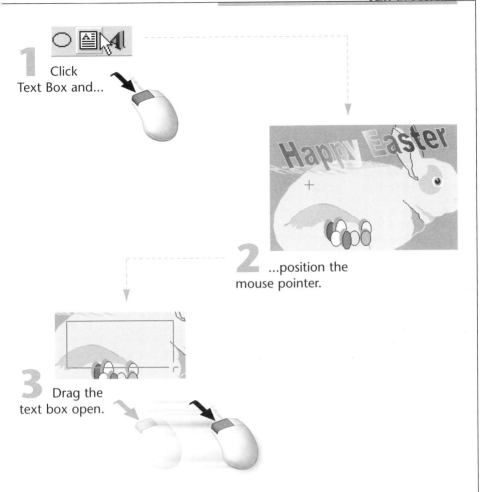

1 Click Text Box and...

2 ...position the mouse pointer.

3 Drag the text box open.

The text box now looks like this, with the cursor flashing inside it. You could enter your text now, but let's jazz things up a bit – after all, Easter comes but once a year. We'll choose a suitable font and make it larger. Then we'll centre the contents of the text box and type in the text.

263

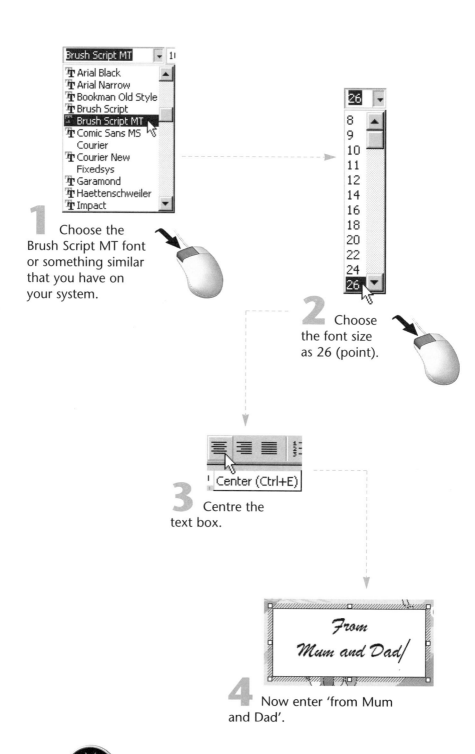

1 Choose the Brush Script MT font or something similar that you have on your system.

2 Choose the font size as 26 (point).

Center (Ctrl+E)

3 Centre the text box.

From
Mum and Dad/

4 Now enter 'from Mum and Dad'.

The Easter Greeting looks wonderful doesn't it? Or perhaps not. The white of the text box is a bit of a nuisance. How can we get rid of it? It's easy, knowing what you do already! We'll choose No Fill for the fill area, making it transparent. To make the border disappear, we'll choose No Line as the Line Color. Remember, when you are editing a text box, it must always be selected. You can see that it is by the sizing handles on its edges.

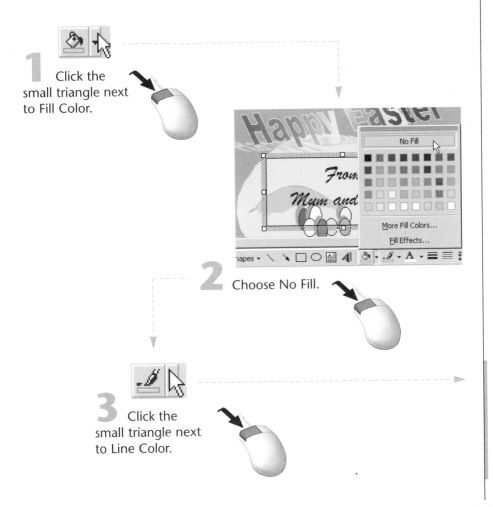

1 Click the small triangle next to Fill Color.

2 Choose No Fill.

3 Click the small triangle next to Line Color.

265

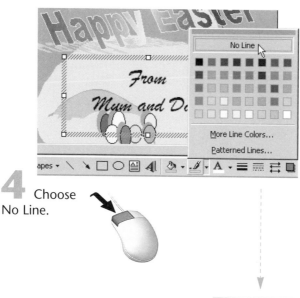

4 Choose No Line.

5 We wish you a 'Happy Easter'.

Try creating your own pictures using Clip Art and WordArt. With a little practice you will discover how much fun you can have.

12

The business letter

What's in this chapter?

Let's talk business. The paperless office still doesn't exist and paperwork inevitably takes up too much time. Bureaucracy is not dead yet! So, to help you make better use of your time, we'll prepare a form that you can use again and again for orders, invoices and letters. And, as we're professionals, we'll have proper stationery, complete with the appropriate watermark.

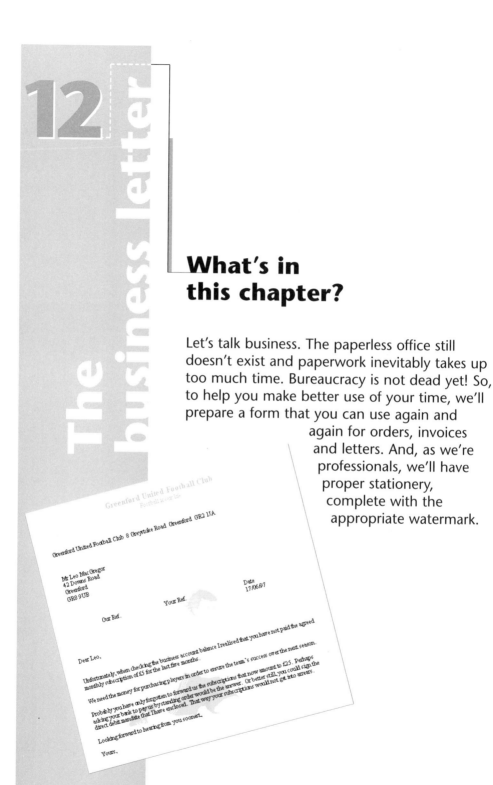

Greenford United Football Club
Football is our life

Greenford United Football Club 8 Greystoke Road Greenford GR2 1JA

Mr Leo MacGregor
42 Downs Road
Greenford
GR8 9UB

Date
17/06/97

Your Ref.

Our Ref.

Dear Leo,

Unfortunately, when checking the business account balance I realised that you have not paid the agreed monthly subscription of £5 for the last five months.

We need the money for purchasing players in order to ensure the team's success over the next season.

Probably you have only forgotten to forward us the subscriptions that now amount to £25. Perhaps asking your bank to pay us by standing order would be the answer. Or better still, you could sign the direct debit mandate that I have enclosed. That way your subscriptions would not get into arrears.

Looking forward to hearing from you soonest.

Yours,

You already know:

You are going to learn:

269

Setting up a recipient's address box

We're now going to design a Club letterhead. It is of course only an example. You could use the same procedure to create 'normal' business stationery.

Header

What's the best game in the world? Football, of course! So we'll invent a football club. At the top of the page we'll enter the club's name, 'Greenford United Football Club', and motto, 'Football is our life'. We'll insert the text in the header, by clicking the View menu and choosing the command Header and Footer.

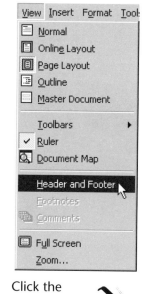

1 Click the View menu and choose the command Header and Footer.

Header

Greenford·United·Football·Club¶
Football·is·our·life‖

2 Enter the name and motto of our football club in the header.

Close

3 Leave the header by clicking Close.

It depends on how you view it!

You can see headers and footers better in Page Layout. You learnt about this view in earlier chapters. Use Page Layout for the next few steps since it makes it easier to carry out the instructions. So change now by clicking the View menu and choosing Page Layout.

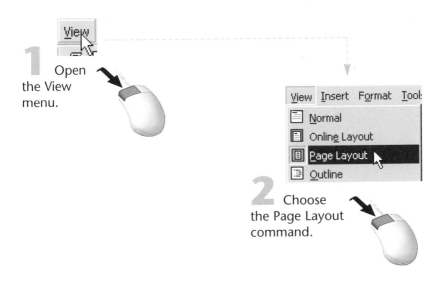

View

1 Open the View menu.

| View | Insert | Format | Tool |

☐ Normal
☐ Online Layout
☐ **Page Layout**
☐ Outline

2 Choose the Page Layout command.

Return to sender

The recipient's address box contains the recipient's name and address.

The next step is to insert the recipient's address box. This is where you type in the name and address of the person you're writing to.

However, first we must indicate that the letter is 'from us'. If you press the ⬅ key precisely as instructed, your letter will fit exactly into a window envelope, provided you fold it correctly. So press the ⬅ key six times and enter the sender's address. Then the Post Office will know who wrote the letter in the event that it cannot be delivered.

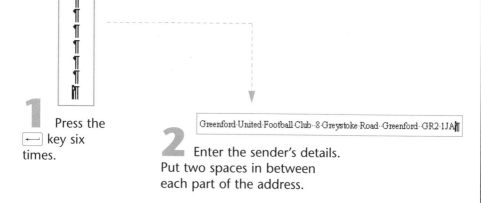

1 Press the ⬅ key six times.

2 Enter the sender's details. Put two spaces in between each part of the address.

Greenford·United·Football·Club··8·Greystoke·Road··Greenford··GR2·1JA¶

Now we'll do the recipient's address box for the recipient's details. Since we're making a template that we'll use over and over again for different letters, we'll enter 'pseudonyms' such as name, street, town, etc.

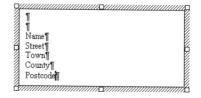

How big should the recipient's address box be? The first line includes the method of despatch. This could by 'Registered Post' or 'By Courier' (1st line). This is not necessary for 'normal' letters. If it's not applicable, the line will remain blank. Then follows a blank line (2nd line) and the recipient's name (3rd line), street (4th line), town (5th line), county (6th line) and post code (7th line). In our example we have seven lines. In practice, it could be more, especially if it's the address of a company.

We'll set the recipient's address box up as a text box. This has the advantage that however large the recipient's address box is, the rest of the letter will not be displaced. The information will only be entered in the text box. Use the button on the Drawing toolbar to create the text box.

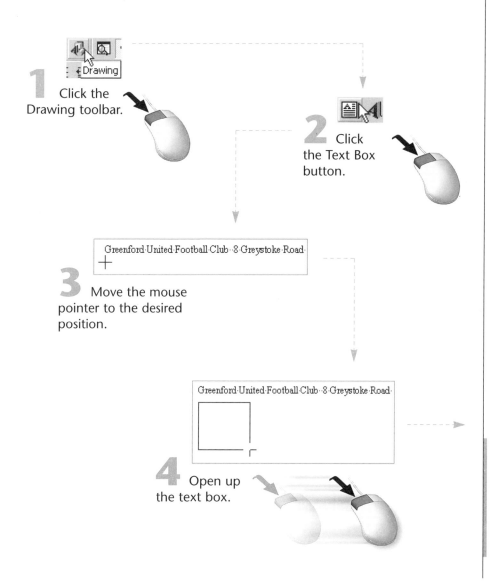

1 Click the Drawing toolbar.

2 Click the Text Box button.

3 Move the mouse pointer to the desired position.

Greenford·United·Football·Club··8·Greystoke·Road·

4 Open up the text box.

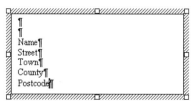

5 Fill in the information.

You can expand or shrink our text box using the sizing handles. The black border is a nuisance. Click the No Fill button under Line Colour to make it

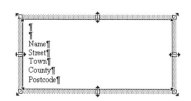

disappear. You can only do this if the text box is selected.

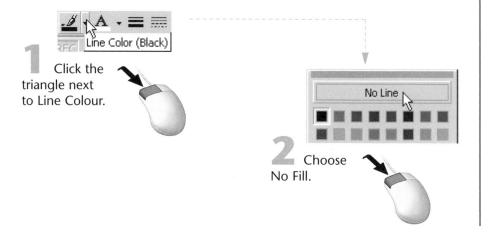

1 Click the triangle next to Line Colour.

2 Choose No Fill.

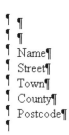

You can hardly tell that the recipient's address box is a text box. However, if you press the ⟵ key several times you will notice that the non printing paragraph symbol (¶) does not appear. In fact it is there, but the text box is covering it. Depending upon the position of your text box, you might just be able to see the left-hand edges of those paragraph symbols beneath it.

¶ ¶
¶ ¶
¶ Name¶
¶ Street¶
¶ Town¶
¶ County¶
¶ Postcode¶
¶

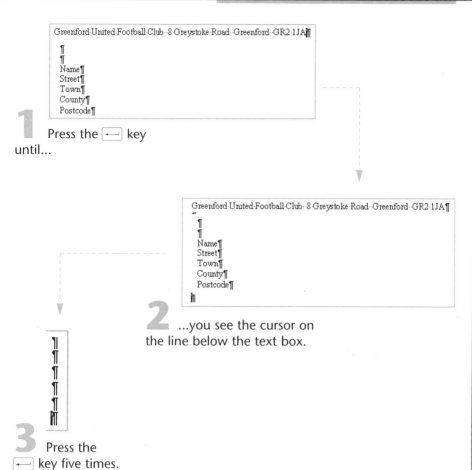

1 Press the ⏎ key until...

2 ...you see the cursor on the line below the text box.

3 Press the ⏎ key five times.

A reference line contains information such as Our Reference, Your Reference and Date. From such details you can always see who wrote a letter or to which letter it refers.

In a proper business letter the reference line follows next. The information is best separated out using tabs.

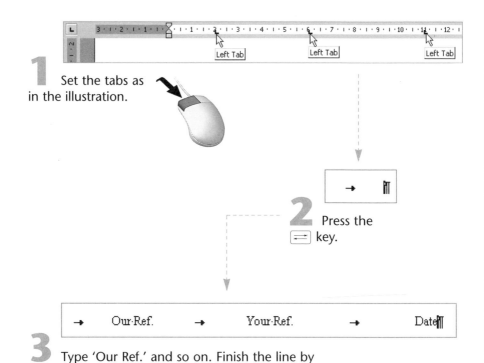

1 Set the tabs as in the illustration.

2 Press the ⇥ key.

3 Type 'Our Ref.' and so on. Finish the line by pressing the ← key.

Up to date

Since our business letter is only a template, we don't have to enter anything in the reference line. The only exception is the date. We will now set this so that each time the letter is opened it automatically shows the correct date.

1 Press the ⇥ key three times.

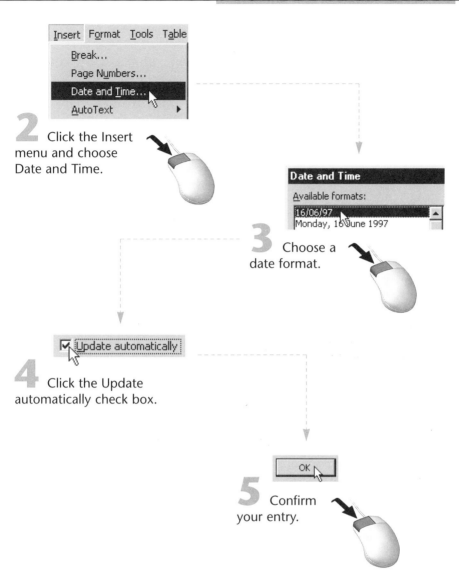

Insert Format Tools Table

Break...
Page Numbers...
Date and Time...
AutoText   ▶

2 Click the Insert menu and choose Date and Time.

Date and Time

Available formats:

16/06/97
Monday, 16 June 1997

3 Choose a date format.

☑ Update automatically

4 Click the Update automatically check box.

OK

5 Confirm your entry.

Now the correct date will appear each time you open the letter. Tomorrow, next week, next year or next century, Word will always get it right, provided your computer is keeping time properly.

Greenford United Football Club
Football is our life

Greenford United Football Club 8 Greystoke Road Greenford GR2 1JA

Name
Street
Town
County
Postcode

Our Ref.   Your Ref.   Date
                                                        16/06/97

Creating a watermark

We would like to create a watermark. Letterheads used to have watermarks stamped into the paper. With Word you can have a do-it-yourself watermark. What would be more appropriate for a football club than a footballer watermark? You can find a suitable candidate from among the sports people graphics by clicking the Insert menu and choosing Picture/Clip Art. To get a better overview of the watermark – and the business letter – reduce the size using the Zoom factor. This makes editing the graphic considerably easier.

1 Reduce the Zoom factor.

2 Click the Insert menu and choose Picture...

3 ...then Clip Art.

4 Make sure the Clip Art tab is foremost.

279

```
(All Categories)
Academic
Animals
Buildings
Cartoons
Entertainment
Gestures
Household
Industry
People at Work
Plants
Screen Beans
Shapes
Signs
Sports & Leisure
Transportation
```

5 You'll find our sportsperson in the Sports & Leisure category.

soccer

6 Choose the soccer Clip Art graphic from among the sports.

The Clip Art graphic will now be in your document. Click it and position the mouse pointer in the centre. The mouse pointer changes to a cross-hairs. Now you can move the footballer about on the letterhead. If you point the mouse pointer at one of the sizing handles, you can change the footballer's size in the directions indicated by the arrows.

We must now tell Word that this graphic is to be a watermark. Click the Format menu and choose Picture. Click the Picture tab. Select Watermark under Image Control. Word now converts the graphic's colour and contrast to look like a watermark.

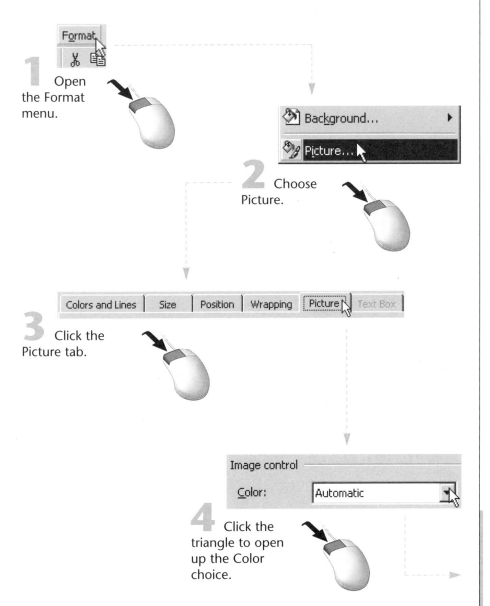

1 Open the Format menu.

2 Choose Picture.

Background... ▶

Picture...

3 Click the Picture tab.

| Colors and Lines | Size | Position | Wrapping | Picture | Text Box |

Image control

Color: Automatic

4 Click the triangle to open up the Color choice.

281

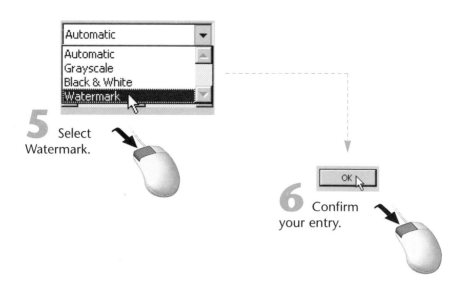

5 Select Watermark.

6 Confirm your entry.

Now the picture looks like a watermark. It has become paler in colour. However, there are still one or two more things to do. If you were to type in text, this would only appear above and below the graphic, but text must be able to run over a watermark. Click the

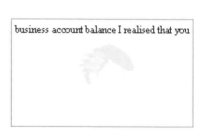

business account balance I realised that you

Format menu and choose the Picture command to determine how

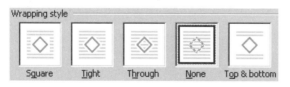

the text should wrap around the graphic. If you choose None, the text is superimposed on the picture. 'Tight' is also an interesting variation. This makes the text follow the contours of the picture exactly. However, in the case of a watermark, the text must be superimposed.

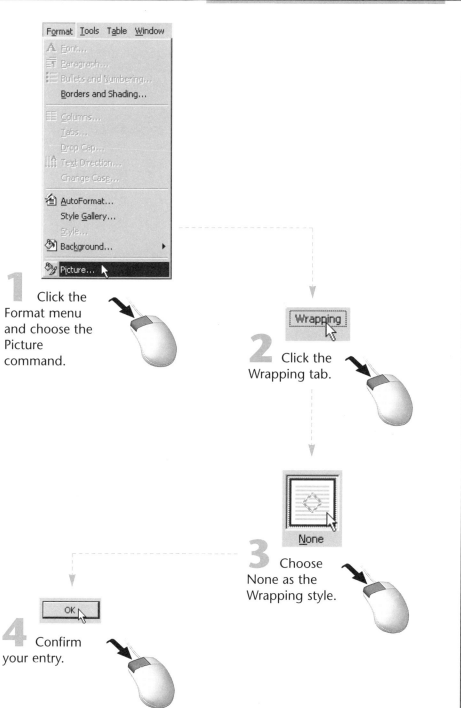

1 Click the Format menu and choose the Picture command.

2 Click the Wrapping tab.

3 Choose None as the Wrapping style.

4 Confirm your entry.

283

In front of and behind the text

Just one more step, and our letterhead is finished. Text would disappear under the picture, and would be pretty hard to read. So we have to tell Word that text must appear in front of the graphic.

Draw ▾ On the Drawing toolbar you'll find the Draw button.

With the Order command you can choose background or foreground. The picture has to be brought behind the text in this case. Remember that the footballer must be selected.

- 🔳 Bring to Front
- 🔳 Send to Back
- 🔳 Bring Forward
- 🔳 Send Backward
- 🔳 Bring in Front of Text
- 🔳 Send Behind Text

Our Ref.   Your Ref.   Date
                                               16/06/97

Dear Leo,

Unfortunately, when check⸱⸱ₒ⸱   siness ⸱   ⸱real⸱ l that you have not paid the agreed
monthly subscription of £5 ⸱ ⸱t⸱ ⸱ ⸱ t five ⸱

We need the money for purchasing players⸱   ⸱e the team's success over the next season.

Probably you have only forgotten to f⸱   ⸱ptions that now amount to £25. Perhaps
asking your bank ⸱⸱ ⸱   ⸱y stand⸱   ⸱nswer. Or better still, you could sign the
direct debit mar⸱   ⸱are e⸱   ⸱criptions would not get into arrears.

Looking forward to hea⸱   ⸱nest,

Yours,

Our Ref.   Your Ref.   Date
                                               16/06/97

Dear Leo,

Unfortunately, when checking the business account balance I realised that you have not paid the agreed monthly subscription of £5 for the last five months.

We need the money for purchasing players in order to ensure the team's success over the next season.

Probably you have only forgotten to forward us the subscriptions that now amount to £25. Perhaps asking your bank to pay us by standing order would be the answer. Or better still, you could sign the direct debit mandate that I have enclosed. That way your subscriptions would not get into arrears.

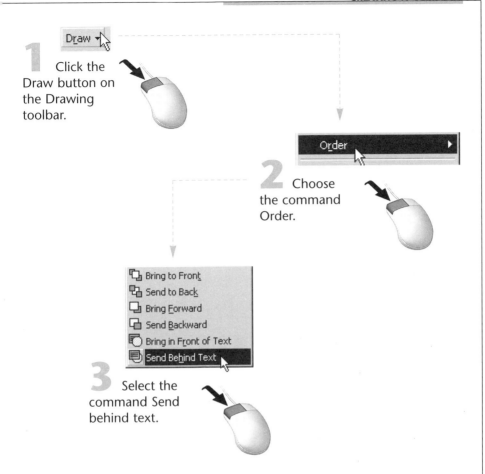

1 Click the Draw button on the Drawing toolbar.

2 Choose the command Order.

3 Select the command Send behind text.

Creating a template

We would like to use our document again and again, but we don't want to have to create the header, recipient's address box and watermark every time. So we'll simply store it as a template to be brought out whenever required. Word has a separate file type for templates. This is divided into different sections, like a binder that has different categories. Letters & Faxes is a suitable section for our

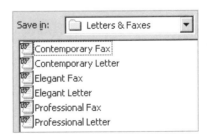

285

business letter. Word's ready-made templates for various letters and faxes are stored here. Save our club letterhead in the normal way. Only when it comes to specifying the file type, choose Document Template instead of Word Document. We'll choose 'Club Letterhead' as the file name.

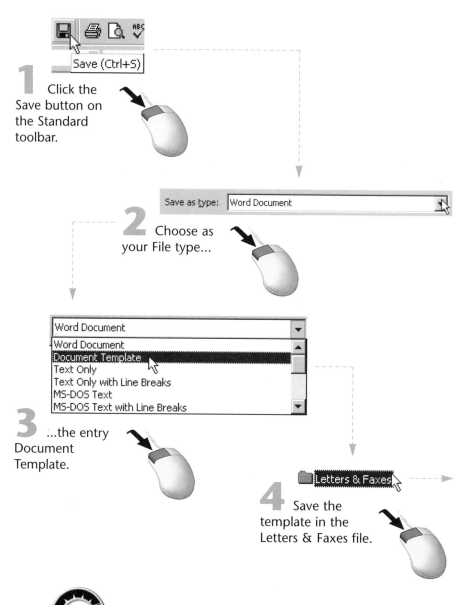

Save (Ctrl+S)

1 Click the Save button on the Standard toolbar.

Save as type: Word Document

2 Choose as your File type...

Word Document
Word Document
Document Template
Text Only
Text Only with Line Breaks
MS-DOS Text
MS-DOS Text with Line Breaks

3 ...the entry Document Template.

Letters & Faxes

4 Save the template in the Letters & Faxes file.

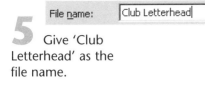

5 Give 'Club Letterhead' as the file name.

6 Save your data.

Working with a template

The club letterhead can be called up at any time. If you would like to write a letter, simply open the template and type in the text. If you want to save a letter to a person, save it as a normal document.

Open the template by clicking the File menu and choosing New. Then click the tab (in this case Letters & Faxes) of the properties sheet where you stored your template.

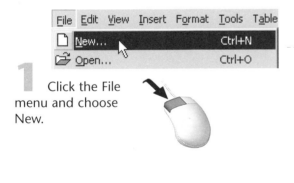

1 Click the File menu and choose New.

2 Click the Letters & Faxes tab to bring it to the fore.

287

Club
Letterhead

Contemporary
Fax

Contemporary
Letter

Elegant Letter

Envelope
Wizard

Fax Wizard

3 Double-click
Club Letterhead...

Greenford United Football Club
Football is our life

Greenford United Football Club 8 Greystoke Road Greenford GR2 1JA

Name
Street
Town
County
Postcode

Our Ref.   Your Ref.   Date
17.06.97

4 ...and the business letter appears on
the screen. All you need do now is type in
the text.

The Word Trainer

Our Ref.   Your Ref.   Date
16/06/97

Dear Leo,

Unfortunately, when checking the business account balance I realised that you have not paid the agreed monthly subscription of £5 for the last five months.

We need the money for purchasing players in order to ensure the team's success over the next season.

Probably you have only forgotten to forward us the subscriptions that now amount to £25. Perhaps asking your bank to pay us by standing order would be the answer. Or better still, you could sign the direct debit mandate that I have enclosed. That way your subscriptions would not get into arrears.

Looking forward to hearing from you soonest,

Yours,

Jo Carter

Enter the above text to check whether all the steps have been carried out correctly and to test whether your watermark appears as it should. Try incorporating watermarks yourself. Store the following example letters as templates before entering the text.

Red Lion Lager
The King of Beers

Red Lion Lager 3 Topers Lane Kingstown K3 FJ2

Name
Street
Town
County
Postcode

Your Ref./Letter dated	Our Ref.	Direct Dial	Date
03.03.98	Tr.	300311	27.05.98

Dear Mr Cooper

Thank you for your letter. We were very impressed with your design for a new can for our lager. I have forwarded your idea to our packaging department. If you have any more ideas on how to promote Red Lion Lager we would be very pleased to hear from you.

Yours sincerely,

Richard Hart

Sparkes Sparkling Wines

Sparkes Sparkling Wines 110 East Street Winechester WN1 4DG

Mr Dale Drinkwater
56 Chestnut Avenue
Bridgetown
BT2 7EG

Price List

Dear Mr Drinkwater,

Thank you for your interest in our products. Here are our prices per bottle:

Sparkes	white	£7.50
Sparkes	red	£6.75
Sparkes	rosé	£7.99
Sparkes	superior	£11.50
Sparkes	special	£10.00
Sparkes	elite	£14.00
Allbright	dry	£9.50
Allbright	low alcohol	£6.90

Yours sincerely,

Andrew Champers

13

Let's write a book

What's in this chapter?

Stay cool! We're not really going to write a novel. However, this chapter will be useful to you even if you're not a Dickens. It's about footnotes, those additional remarks at the bottom of the page. You'll also learn how to enlarge the initial capital letter at the start of a chapter to make it stand out. What happens when you write more than one page? You'll need page numbers, of course!

You already know:

You are going to learn:

Footnotes

Footnotes are often used in research papers and in company reports to provide further explanation at the bottom of the page.

Endnotes are used when the additional information is collected together at the end of a text that extends over several sides.

You know of course what footnotes are. They are frequently used in books and contain additional information that appears at the bottom of the page.

Jeffrey Archer[1]

In our example we have written 'Jeffrey Archer'. In the footnote we'll say that he is an English author. The View that you have selected is all-important for what you see when creating a footnote. To see the same effect as in our next few steps, choose Normal View. In Page Layout, footnote input would look like this.

[1] English Author

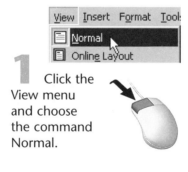

1 Click the View menu and choose the command Normal.

I was recently in Cambridge where I had lunch with Jeffrey Archer. Later Mary joined us.

2 Input the text.

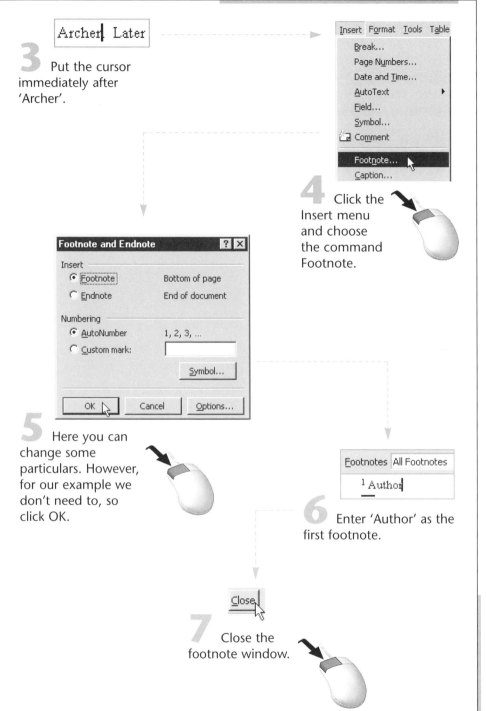

3 Put the cursor immediately after 'Archer'.

Insert Format Tools Table
Break...
Page Numbers...
Date and Time...
AutoText ▶
Field...
Symbol...
Comment
Footnote...
Caption...

4 Click the Insert menu and choose the command Footnote.

Footnote and Endnote ? ✕

Insert
○ Footnote   Bottom of page
○ Endnote   End of document

Numbering
○ AutoNumber   1, 2, 3, ...
○ Custom mark: [   ]
                    Symbol...

OK   Cancel   Options...

5 Here you can change some particulars. However, for our example we don't need to, so click OK.

Footnotes All Footnotes
¹ Author

6 Enter 'Author' as the first footnote.

Close

7 Close the footnote window.

295

Behind 'Archer' there is now a small superscript '1'. This means that the first footnote is here. If you move the mouse pointer to the number, the footnote contents are displayed in a yellow box.

Editing footnotes

In our example we want to add to the footnote. So far, it reads 'Author'. This needs to be changed to 'English author'. To edit a footnote, click the View menu and choose the Footnotes command. It's even quicker if you use the mouse. A double click on the superscript '1' behind 'Archer' takes you to the footnote window. Here you can make your change.

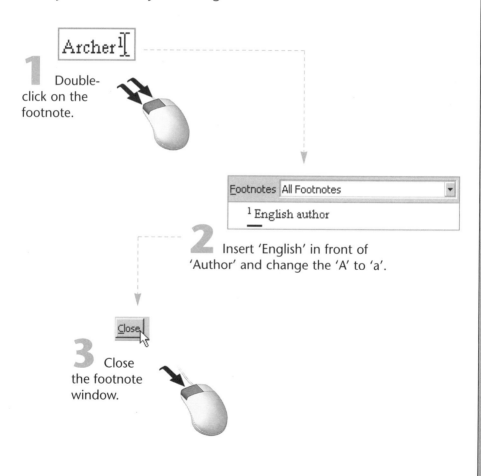

1 Double-click on the footnote.

Footnotes | All Footnotes

¹ English author

2 Insert 'English' in front of 'Author' and change the 'A' to 'a'.

Close

3 Close the footnote window.

If you move the mouse pointer to the first footnote, the new contents are displayed. Now let's move on to the second footnote. Proceed exactly as for the first footnote. In our example, place the cursor directly after 'Mary', then click the Insert menu and give the command Footnote. Enter the second text. In this way you can create as many footnotes as you consider necessary.

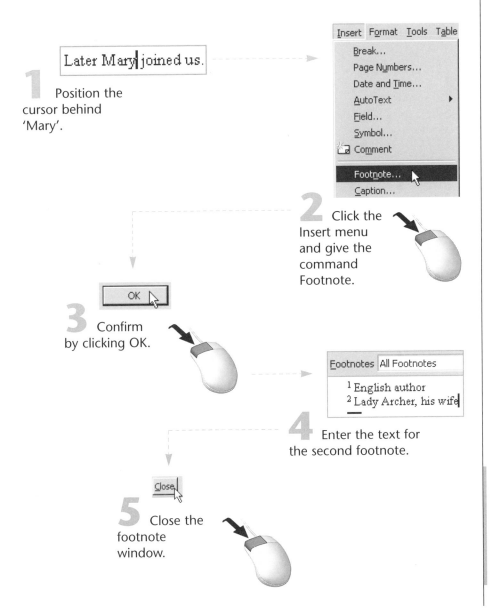

Later Mary joined us.

1 Position the cursor behind 'Mary'.

Insert Format Tools Table

Break...
Page Numbers...
Date and Time...
AutoText ▶
Field...
Symbol...
Comment
Footnote...
Caption...

2 Click the Insert menu and give the command Footnote.

OK

3 Confirm by clicking OK.

Footnotes | All Footnotes

¹ English author
² Lady Archer, his wife

4 Enter the text for the second footnote.

Close

5 Close the footnote window.

Deleting footnotes

Nothing is easier than removing footnotes. Simply select the footnote and press the $\boxed{\text{Delete}}$ key. This results in both the footnote and its contents being deleted at the same time. However, Word is even cleverer than you think. As soon as you remove a footnote, it renumbers the remaining footnotes in the correct sequence. The second footnote therefore becomes the first.

Jeffrey Archer[1]

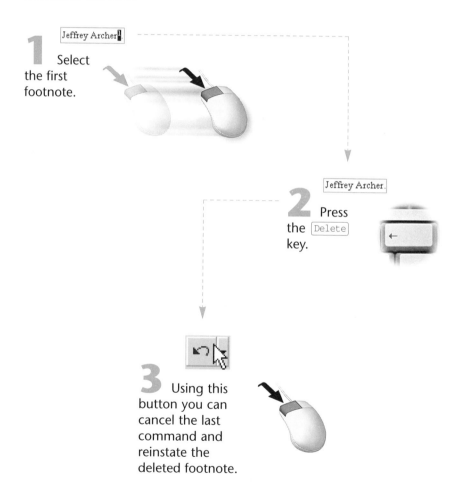

1 Select the first footnote.

2 Press the $\boxed{\text{Delete}}$ key.

3 Using this button you can cancel the last command and reinstate the deleted footnote.

Seeing footnotes

It is difficult to see the footnotes in the text. Apart from the superscript numbers there's nothing to see because you are still in Normal View. If you change the View to Page Layout, the footnotes will be displayed at the end of the page.

If you click Print Preview to check the appearance of your document, you can also see the footnotes. Move the magnifying glass to the bottom of the page and click to magnify the text. After you have checked that all is OK, leave the Print Preview by clicking the Close button or pressing the Esc key.

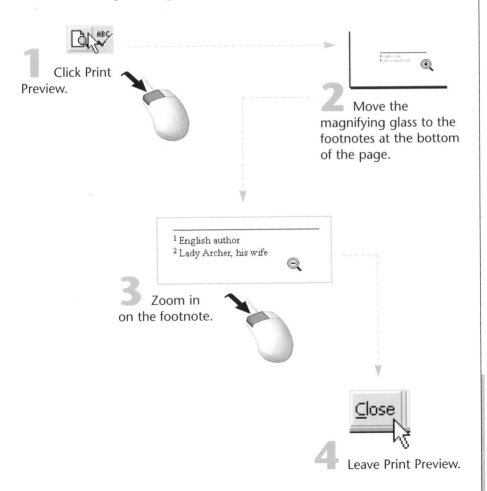

Click Print Preview.

2 Move the magnifying glass to the footnotes at the bottom of the page.

[1] English author
[2] Lady Archer, his wife

3 Zoom in on the footnote.

Close

4 Leave Print Preview.

Repeating commands

Now we're going to write our book! Well, not really. Just one page, in fact, and not even that. We only need to write one sentence, and then we can fill a whole page with it in next to no time. So, we write the sentence, copy the text and insert it again. Then we'll see what happens next!

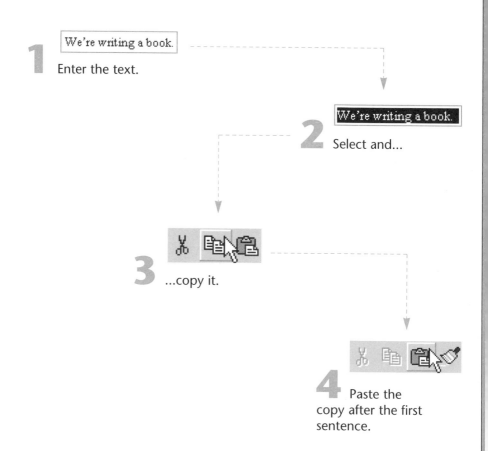

1 Enter the text.

We're writing a book.

2 Select and...

We're writing a book.

3 ...copy it.

4 Paste the copy after the first sentence.

Again and again

The sentence is now in the Clipboard, the computer's short-term memory. It will stay there until you copy (or cut) something new. So you only need to click the Paste button repeatedly. However, it's just as quick to use the keyboard. If you press the ⌐F4⌐ key, the last command that you gave is repeated (in the Edit menu this is done using the Repeat command).

> We're writing a book. We're writing a

1 Repeat the command by pressing the ⌐F4⌐ key.

| Page 2 | Sec 1 | | 2/2 |

2 You can see on the Status bar when you reach the second page.

Inserting page numbers

In our example we have two pages of text. Page numbers are useful if your document has several pages.

Click the Insert menu and choose the command Page Numbers. Here you can decide where the numbers should appear: on the left, on the right or in the middle. They need not

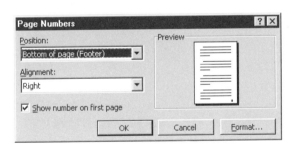

be at the bottom of the page, but could equally well be at the top. The black dot in the Preview shows you where the number will appear when you click OK.

301

Page numbering can start at any number. Click Insert then choose Page Numbers. Click the Format button and enter the desired number in the Start at box.

1 Click Insert then choose the Page Numbers command.

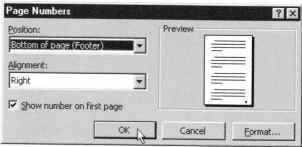

2 Confirm by clicking OK.

Seeing the page numbers

In Normal View you cannot see the page numbers. In Page Layout they are at the bottom of the page. Print Preview again comes in useful. Here we can see whether the page numbers are correctly placed. Zoom in on them with the magnifying glass.

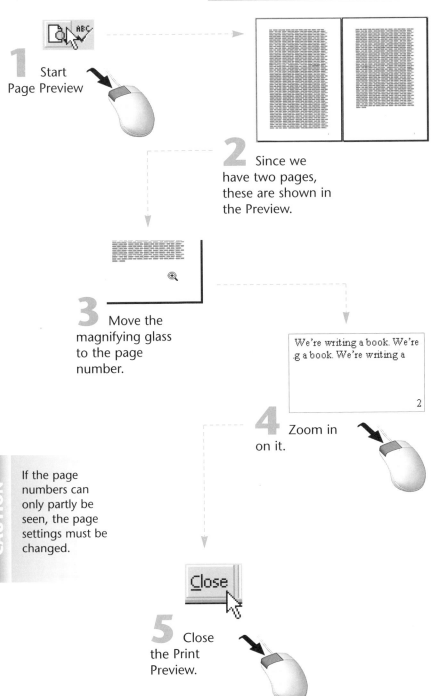

1 Start
Page Preview

2 Since we
have two pages,
these are shown in
the Preview.

3 Move the
magnifying glass
to the page
number.

We're writing a book. We're
.g a book. We're writing a

2

4 Zoom in
on it.

If the page
numbers can
only partly be
seen, the page
settings must be
changed.

Close

5 Close
the Print
Preview.

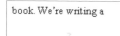

book. We're writing a

Here you can see why it is a good idea to check the layout first using Print Preview. Only half of the page number is showing. This means that you would get the same result if you were to print the page. When you insert page numbers, Word automatically places them in the Footer (or at the top in the header).

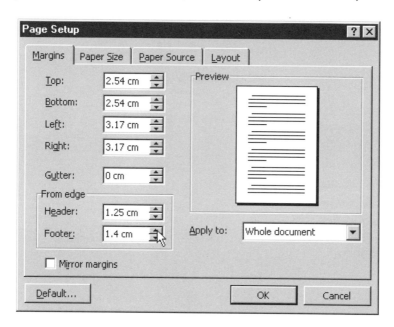

Click the File menu and choose Page Setup to set the borders of your document. Word gives you standard settings. If you increase the space taken by the footer, the page numbers will appear in full. So change the settings if you need to. Click the Default button to indicate that the new settings should always apply from now on.

Creating drop capitals

Drop capitals are an eye-catching way to start a text. They can either be contained within the paragraph or can be placed outside the left border of the text.

Drop capitals can only be inserted in Page Layout.

You know about initials from posh handkerchiefs that have their owner's monograms embroidered onto them. In Word there is a way of emphasising the initial capital letter of a paragraph.

Click Format and choose the Drop Cap command. Here you have a choice. Dropped makes the letter appear within the text, which automatically flows around it.

With In Margin, the initial letter appears outside the text. With None, you can shrink the initial capital again.

1 Click Format and choose the Drop Cap command.

Dropped

2 Choose an initial letter from the Position layout boxes.

The Word Trainer

Exercise in the use of footnotes

Fred Rivers was diving off the coast of Flaminguna. There he saw three sharks. He escaped from two of them, but the third one got him!

1 Enter the example paragraph.
Change to Normal View if you need to.

Fred Rivers[1] ... ... Flaminguna[2] ... ... sharks[3] ... ...

2 Insert footnotes after the words...

Footnotes | All Footnotes | ▾ | Close

[1] British marine biologist
[2] Island off the coast of South America
[3] Marine animal

3 ... and type in the text for each.

Flaminguna[2]

4 Select the 2nd footnote...

Fred Rivers[1] ... ... Flaminguna ... ... sharks[2] ... ...

5 ... and delete it using the Delete key.

Exercise in the use of drop capitals

1 Click the Format menu and choose the Drop Cap command.

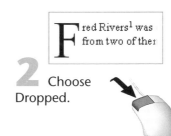

2 Choose Dropped.

What's in this chapter?

Long live statistics! Numbers can be very dry,
though. Pour youself a nice glass of water and
liven up your statistics by using diagrams to
represent them. If all the information can be
seen at a glance, there's no need for pages of
text. Facts become
clearer and easier to
retain with the help of
circles, bars and
symbols.

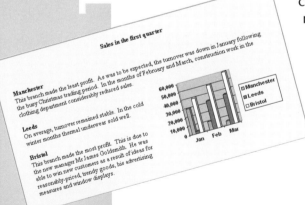

You already know:

You are going to learn:

309

Inserting a chart

Charts are very useful for presenting figures. Word comes with an application for this purpose by the name of Microsoft (MS) Graph.

To insert a chart, choose the Picture command from the Insert menu, then choose Chart. This takes you to the MS Graph application.

Sales in the first quarter

Manchester
This branch made the least profit. As was to be expected, the turnover was down in January following the busy Christmas trading period. In the months of February and March, construction work in the clothing department considerably reduced sales.

Leeds
On average, turnover remained stable. In the cold winter months thermal underwear sold well.

Bristol
This branch made the most profit. This is due to the new manager Mr James Goldsmith. He was able to win new customers as a result of ideas for reasonably-priced, trendy goods, his advertising measures and window displays.

---

1 Type in the text. We'll immediately link a chart to it.

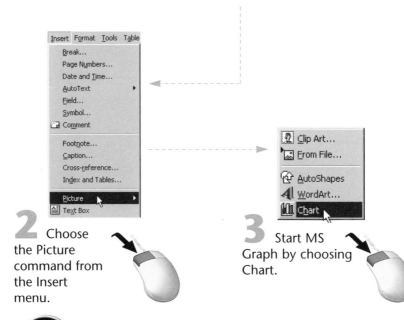

2 Choose the Picture command from the Insert menu.

3 Start MS Graph by choosing Chart.

Editing the table

The next step is to enter the data. You'll see a table and behind it a chart that is related to the table in the foreground. The values for it are to be found in the table cells.

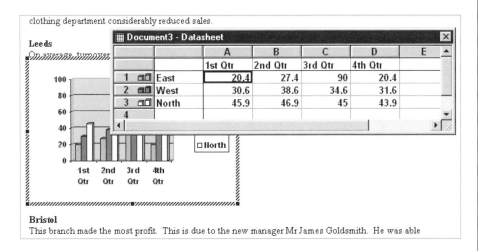

If the cursor is over the cells, the mouse pointer changes to a white cross. You can remove the contents of a cell by clicking it and pressing the `Delete` key. However, you can also simply overwrite the contents. First we'll type in the cities and months in our example.

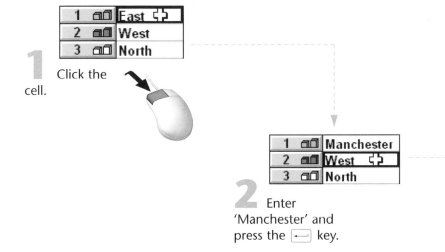

1 Click the cell.

2 Enter 'Manchester' and press the ⏎ key.

311

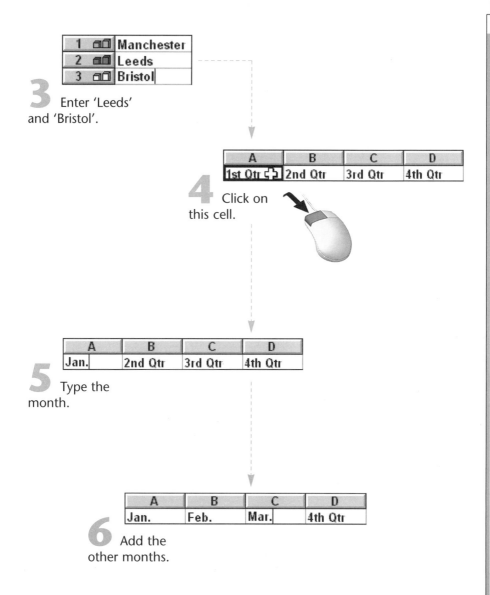

1	⬜	Manchester
2	⬜	Leeds
3	⬜	Bristol|

3 Enter 'Leeds' and 'Bristol'.

A	B	C	D
1st Qtr ⊞	2nd Qtr	3rd Qtr	4th Qtr

4 Click on this cell.

A	B	C	D
Jan.|	2nd Qtr	3rd Qtr	4th Qtr

5 Type the month.

A	B	C	D
Jan.	Feb.	Mar.|	4th Qtr

6 Add the other months.

Since we've only got figures for three months at the moment, we don't need the fourth column – column D. Simply click on the D to select the entire column. Press the Delete key to delete the contents.

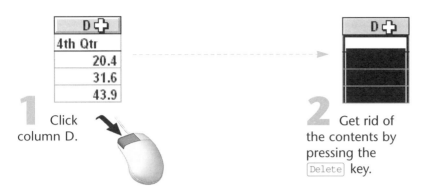

1 Click column D.

2 Get rid of the contents by pressing the `Delete` key.

Facts, facts, facts

Now we come to our company's profits for the quarter. Enter the figures in the cells. During input, watch what happens to the chart. When you have finished, leave the MS Graph application, simply by clicking in the Word document.

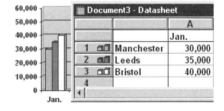

	Jan.	Feb.	Mar.
Manchester	30,000	10,000	5,000
Leeds	35,000	32,500	35,000
Bristol	40,000	50,000	60,000

1 Enter the figures in the cells.

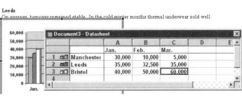

2 Click anywhere in the Word document outside MS Graph.

Editing a chart

It must flow!

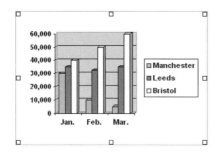

The table vanishes from your screen. The chart is now in your document. The figures were correctly entered. However, we need to edit the chart a little, so click on it. You should be able to see the sizing handles around the border of the graphic. The text either side of the graphic is not flowing properly – it is either above or below it. You could choose Object from the Format menu. However, we'll do it another way. If you click the right mouse button a menu opens. Choose Format Object from here. Click the Wrapping tab so that this properties sheet comes to the fore. If you choose Square as the Wrapping style, the text flows round the chart.

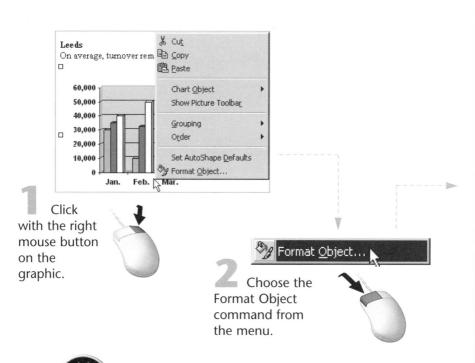

1 Click with the right mouse button on the graphic.

2 Choose the Format Object command from the menu.

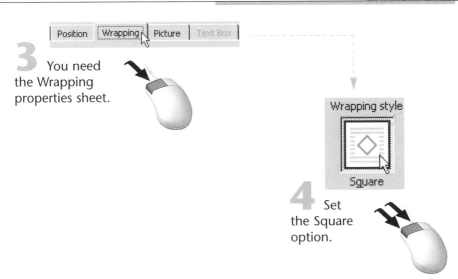

3 You need the Wrapping properties sheet.

4 Set the Square option.

Moving the diagram

If the diagram does not look right where it is, just click it. Beside the mouse pointer are cross-hairs with which you can move your graphic around in the document. Hold the mouse button down and move the

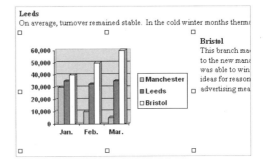

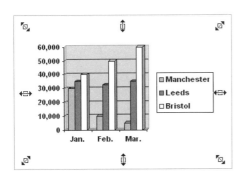

graphic wherever you want. If the chart looks too small on the screen, position the mouse pointer on one of the sizing handles. You can enlarge or reduce the graphic in the direction of the arrows.

315

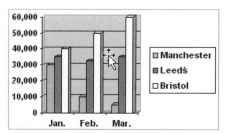

1 Click the graphic.

the busy Christmas trading period. In the months of February and March, construction work in the clothing department considerably reduced sales.

Leeds
On average, turnover remained stable. In the cold winter months thermal underwear sold well.

Bristol
This branch made the most profit. This is due to the new manager Mr James Goldsmith. He was able to win new customers as a result of ideas for reasonably-priced, trendy goods, his advertising measures and window displays.

2 Move the chart...

Manchester
This branch made the least profit. As was to be expected, the turnover was down in January following the busy Christmas trading period. In the months of February and March, construction work in the clothing department considerably reduced sales.

Leeds
On average, turnover remained stable. In the cold winter months thermal underwear sold well.

Bristol
This branch made the most profit. This is due to the new manager Mr James Goldsmith. He was able to win new customers as a result of ideas for reasonably-priced, trendy goods, his advertising measures and window displays.

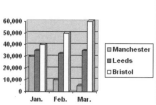

3 ...to this position in the text.

Bars, circles, dots ...

You're spoilt for choice if you want to change the appearance of your chart. For example, you could change the Chart Type. With MS Graph active, go to the Chart Type button on the Standard toolbar. Click the black triangle next to it and you'll be offered a wealth of possibilities. However, they don't all make the chart easier to read.

Changing the figures is a piece of cake

In our example, let's pretend that an error is found on checking the figures. The figures from the Bristol branch have been 'cooked'. There is a great outcry at the branch. The turnover for March has been set too high for cosmetic reasons. The branch manager is sacked and now plans to start a hot dog stand.

The true facts must be recorded, but it's no big deal. We do not have to insert a new chart, but can use the old one. Double-click the graphic to start MS Graph and the familiar table appears. Simply change the figures. In the background you can see the chart changing. Click in the Word document to leave MS Graph again.

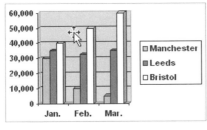

1 Start MS Graph by double-clicking the chart.

Mar.
5,000
35,000
60,000

2 Click the '60,000' for the month of March at the Bristol branch.

317

Mar.
5,000
35,000
10,000

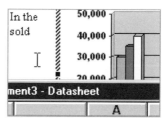

3 Change the turnover to '10,000'.

4 Click in the Word document to leave MS Graph again.

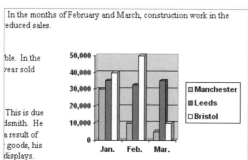

In the months of February and March, construction work in the 'educed sales.

ble. In the year sold

This is due dsmith. He a result of goods, his displays.

5 The March turnover for the Bristol branch now looks rather different.

The Word Trainer

This exercise will make you even more confident about working with charts. We'll also show you some new tricks.

New figures

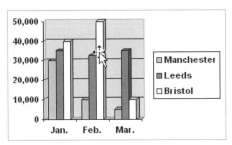

1 Start MS Graph by double-clicking in the chart.

D
Apr.
10,000
40,000
30,000

2 The figures for another month are now available at the office. Fill in the new values in column D.

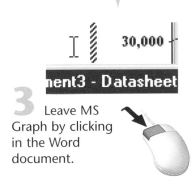

3 Leave MS Graph by clicking in the Word document.

319

The new figures are automatically incorporated in the chart. You could also add new data in the same way. If the graphic becomes too

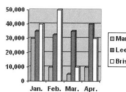

Manchester
This branch made the least profit. As was to be expected, the turnover was down in January following the busy Christmas trading period. In the months of February and March, construction work in the clothing department considerably reduced sales.

Leeds
On average, turnover remained stable. In the cold winter months thermal underwear sold well.

Bristol
This branch made the most profit. This is due to the new manager Mr James Goldsmith. He was able to win new customers as a result of ideas for reasonably-priced, trendy goods, his advertising measures and window displays.

small, simply enlarge it using the sizing handles.

A new type of chart

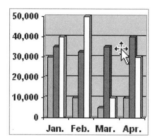

1 You can change the way the figures are represented. Double-click in the chart.

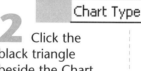

Chart Type

2 Click the black triangle beside the Chart Type button...

3 ...and choose the Bar Chart, for example.

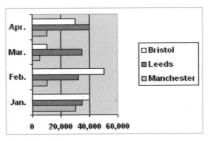

4 If you like, you can try out the other chart types in the same way.

321

What's in this chapter?

You don't have to live with Word's interface just as it is. If you frequently need functions that are not available in the individual toolbars, you can simply insert them. You can create your own menu options, buttons and even shortcut keys. Then you can say: 'This is my Word'. Since we're now Word 'pros', we'll make it even easier to start Word. A double click, and the program appears on the screen. It's easy!

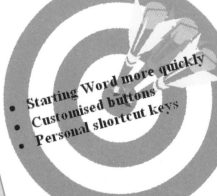

- Starting Word more quickly
- Customised buttons
- Personal shortcut keys

You already know:

You are going to learn:

323

Word as an icon

The Windows interface is called the desktop.

All roads lead to Rome, but some are shorter than others. You just need to know the shortest. The same applies to starting Word. The shortest way would be to have Word as an icon on the Windows 95 desktop.

Microsoft Word

You must have noticed the icons here already. Double-click them, and the program they belong to starts. This works the same for Word. Move the mouse pointer to the Start button. Then click the right mouse button and choose Open. Since Word is a program, double-click Programs. Now you can see the Word icon. Simultaneously hold down the left mouse button and the Ctrl key to drag a copy of the icon to the desktop. There it will stay until you remove it.

1 Position the mouse pointer on Start and click the right mouse button.

Start

Open
Explore
Find...

2 Choose Open.

Programs

3 Open the Programs folder

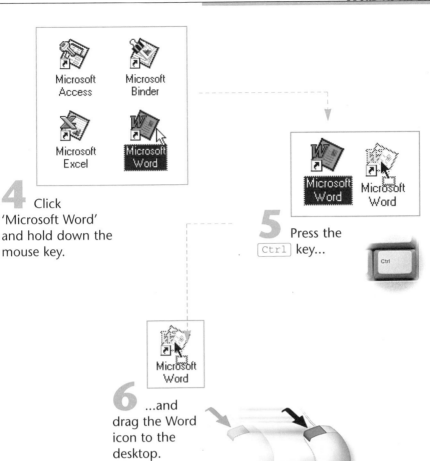

4 Click
'Microsoft Word'
and hold down the
mouse key.

5 Press the
Ctrl key...

6 ...and
drag the Word
icon to the
desktop.

The icon is now on the Windows 95
desktop. Double-click it, and Word
starts. If you hold down the left
mouse button, you can drag the icon
wherever you want.

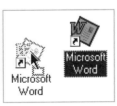

325

Customising a button

In Word you can customise your own buttons. We'll show you how in an example. In the File menu you'll find the command Close. This closes a document without your having to exit Word. If you have several documents open on your screen, you have to close them one at a

time. However, the command Close All does exist. All we have to do is insert it.

Of course, you could also insert other buttons in the same way. You'll find the various commands under Tools/Customize. Here you'll see a number of Categories. You'll find the Close All command under File. While holding the mouse button down, simply drag the command into the Standard toolbar to join the other buttons.

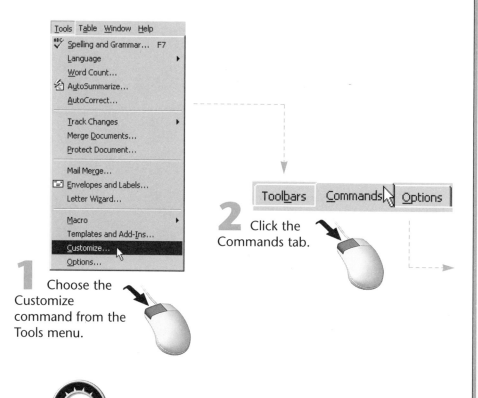

1 Choose the Customize command from the Tools menu.

2 Click the Commands tab.

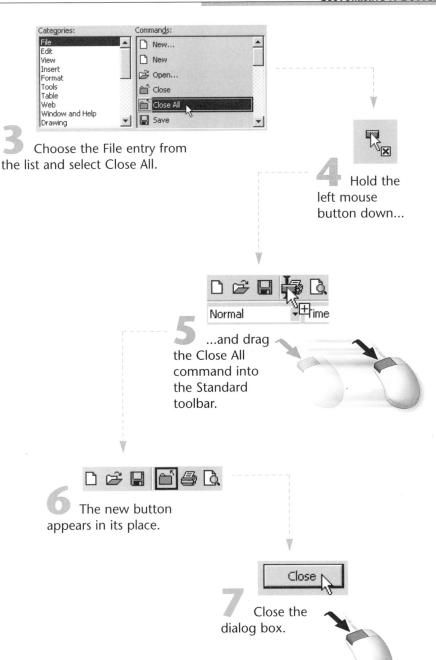

3 Choose the File entry from the list and select Close All.

4 Hold the left mouse button down...

5 ...and drag the Close All command into the Standard toolbar.

6 The new button appears in its place.

7 Close the dialog box.

327

Removing buttons

If you now move the mouse pointer to the new button, Word shows you what it does. If you want to get rid of a button – and that applies to any – you once again choose Customize from the Tools menu. It is sufficient that the Customize

dialog box is open on the screen. It doesn't matter which properties sheet is foremost. Drag the button with the left mouse button held down into the dialog box to delete it from the Standard toolbar.

Creating a menu option

Just as you inserted a new button in the Standard toolbar, you can also insert a command into a menu. We'll take Close All as an example. Once again, choose Customize from the Tools menu and click the Commands tab. Find the command you want – Close All, in this case. Now open the menu into which the command is to be inserted. While holding the mouse key down, drag the command from the Customize dialog box into the opened Menu.

1 Choose the Customize command from the Tools menu and find Close All in the Commands property sheet.

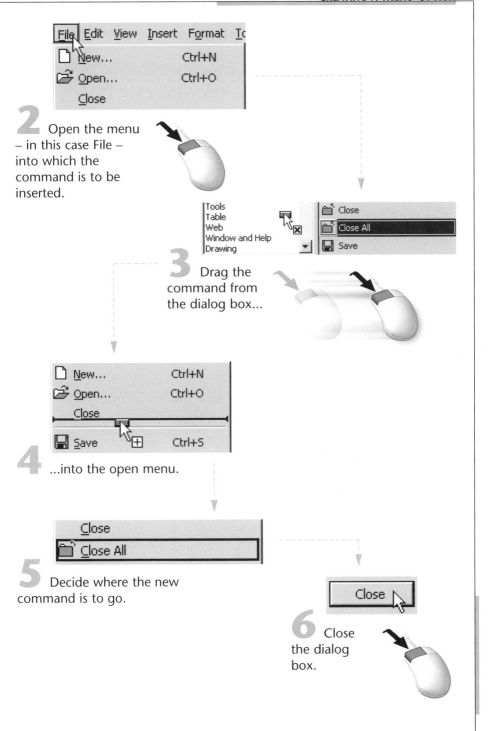

2 Open the menu – in this case File – into which the command is to be inserted.

3 Drag the command from the dialog box...

4 ...into the open menu.

5 Decide where the new command is to go.

6 Close the dialog box.

329

Removing commands from the menu

If you open the File menu, you'll see that the new command has been inserted. If you want to remove a command – any command, that is – you again need the Customize dialog box (choose Customize from the Tools menu). It does not matter

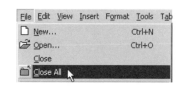

which properties sheet is foremost. Open the menu and drag the

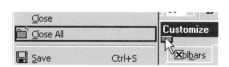

command you want to remove into the dialog box. The command disappears from the menu.

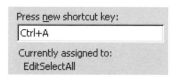

Personal shortcut keys

Word can also satisfy your desire for personal shortcut keys. We'll take as an example once again our Close All command. Choose Customize from the Tools menu and click the Commands

tab. However, this time we'll go one step further. Since we want to decide on a key combination, we'll click Keyboard.

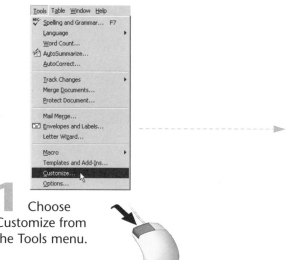

1 Choose Customize from the Tools menu.

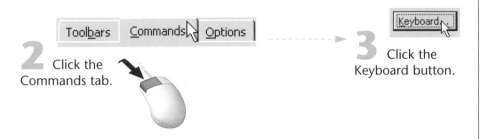

2 Click the Commands tab.

3 Click the Keyboard button.

The various commands are divided into categories here. For our example you need the File entry. The command we require is second from the top in this alphabetical list. We'll choose the key

combination Alt + A for Close All. If the keys have already been assigned to other commands, Word will tell you. Now press the key combination Alt + A simultaneously. When these appear in the 'Press new shortcut key' box, click the Assign button. This means that the shortcut key combination you have chosen will be assigned to the Close All command.

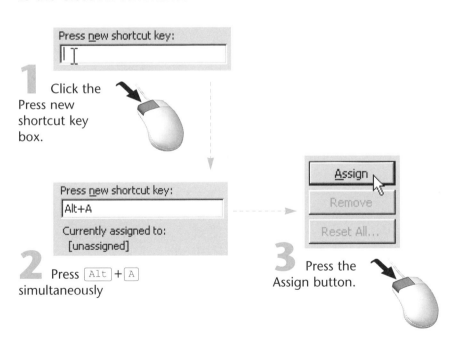

1 Click the Press new shortcut key box.

2 Press Alt + A simultaneously

3 Press the Assign button.

331

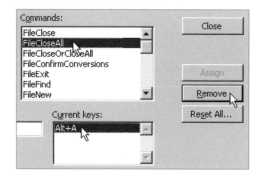

The shortcut key combination now appears under Current keys. Until you change it, these keys belong to this command. In order to delete key combinations, click the command and then click Remove.

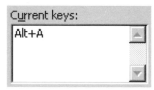

Finally, you need to close both dialog boxes that are open on your screen.

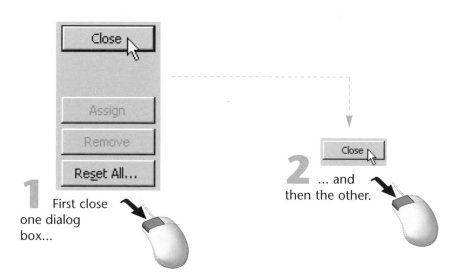

1 First close one dialog box...

2 ... and then the other.

You can now try out the new keys. It's easy to check whether everything is in order. Move the mouse pointer to the appropriate button. If Show Shortcut keys in ScreenTips has been turned on, Word will show you the new shortcut key. Another way would be to open the File menu. The key combination you chose will be displayed after Close All.

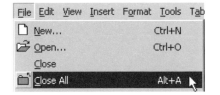

What's in this chapter?

If you can't swim and you're about to drown, you need someone to dive in and pull you out. If there's nobody about, you desperately need a lifebelt. Word offers you lifebelts in the form of various kinds of help. So, if you're having trouble, you could close your eyes and hope for a miracle, or – more sensibly – you could turn to Word's help facilities. There's a lot more to them than you might think!

Installation

Most users don't install Office 97 themselves. If you buy a PC, the dealer generally does it for you. However, if you have to install Word on your own, there's no need to panic. Much will already have been done when Windows 95 was installed – for example, adaptation to your hardware (such as mouse, printer or monitor). And, as you know, Windows 95 is needed for Word 97.

When you insert the CD-ROM, most of the installation happens by itself. The installation program (called Setup) appears on your screen. The recommended functions have already been activated and need only be confirmed.

You can choose between different types of installation. These are: 'standard', 'custom' and 'start from CD'. The standard installation takes up most space on your hard disk. In this case the program is installed automatically. In the case of 'custom', the user-defined version, you indicate only the modules that you wish to install. This is to be recommended if you have a limited amount of space on your hard disk. With Start from CD, you have to run Word from the CD each time. This takes up less space on your hard disk, but working with the program is considerably slower.

Subsequent installation

If you would like to do without some programs when you first install Office 97, this is not a problem. Click the check boxes of the programs you require and a tick confirms that they will be installed. If you remove the tick by clicking, the program will not be installed. If you decide later to deinstall a piece of software, simply insert the CD-ROM and indicate what you want to delete from the hard disk.

Options:		Description:
☑ Microsoft Binder	1806 K	Microsoft Excel will be installed with
☑ Microsoft Excel	15237 K	only the selected options.
☑ Microsoft Word	24624 K	
☑ Microsoft PowerPoint	25047 K	
☑ Microsoft Outlook	23433 K	
☐ Web Page Authoring (HTML)	8474 K	
☑ Data Access	4653 K	
☑ Office Tools	14846 K	Change Option...
☑ Converters and Filters	5497 K	
☑ Getting Results Book	16 K	Select All

Always make sure there is sufficient space on your hard disk. In the case below, there is not enough. It is useless trying to install Office 97, for if you do it will terminate prematurely by itself. To make more space you must think which other programs (games?) you could delete from your hard disk.

| Space required on C: | 115159 K |
| Space available on C: | 344400 K |

Only when you receive this message confirming that the installation has been successfully completed can you start working with Word.

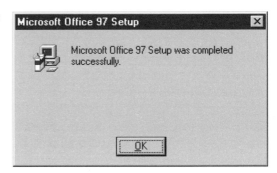

Clipit – your friend and helper

A fun innovation in Word are the jolly little animations that are
at your disposal. If you click on the question mark button, an
Assistant appears. This is 'Clipit', the lively cartoon character
who is there to help you as you work with Word. Take the mouse
pointer to your Assistant and click with the right mouse button to
reveal a menu.

Here you can home in on all kinds of
commands. For example, using Options
you can determine which tips the
Assistant will show you.

Select Animate! to make
your Assistant perform
for you. Go on, try it.

Click Choose Assistant and all kinds of helpers appear. You are spoilt
for choice between Clipit, The Dot, The Genius, Hoverbot, Office
Logo, Mother Nature, Power Pup, Scribble the Cat and Will.

If you decide to change your assistant you will have to insert the
installation CD-ROM again.

Have you still got questions?

If you want to ask Word something, simply click your Assistant. Enter your request and click Search. While you are typing your question, your Assistant is busily making notes. Your request doesn't have to be in the form of a question, but it needs to be phrased so that your Assistant can understand. A key word is usually enough. In this case, 'form letters' was typed in.

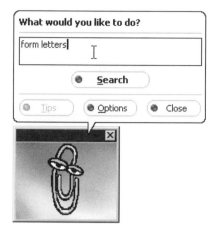

What would you like to do?

 Form letters, envelopes, and labels

 Set up a main document for a mail merge

 Print a document

The result of the search is that several areas are suggested to you as being relevant to your request.

Look for what seems most appropriate. In our example, click 'Form letters, envelopes, and labels', and Word will present you with its information and instructions on the subject.

Form letters, envelopes, and labels

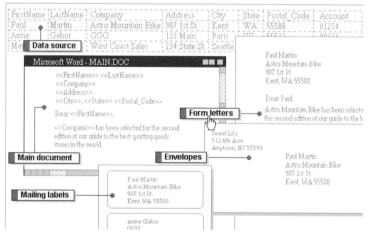

Further help

In Word, there are various additional forms of help that are aimed not just at beginners. Click the Help menu and choose the command Contents AND Index. Click the Contents tab. Here you can find the

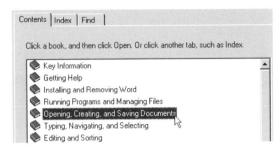

individual help books. Double-click one of them (of course, you can also click once and choose the Open button). You'll be shown a selection of separate subject areas. Once again, double-click one of the subjects, and you'll be shown a detailed explanation of the chosen subject.

Help via the index

In the Index properties sheet (under Help/Contents and Index), you can type in search words relating to subjects on which you need help. If you enter your search word in the box that asks you to 'Type the first few letters of the word you're looking for', you'll see how Word jumps down the list with each letter that you

input, already selecting terms that might be relevant. Click the Display button to read the explanations you require.

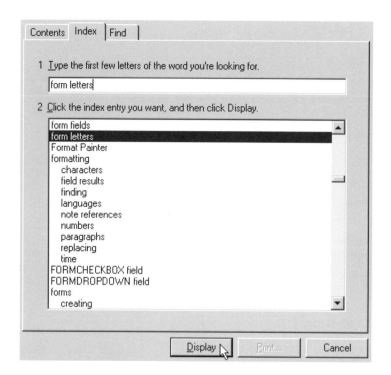

What's This?

One form of help that everyone should know about is 'What's This?', which gives you access to Word's ScreenTips. You can access this facility while you're working by clicking What's This in the Help menu.

 Your mouse pointer acquires a question mark.

If, for example, you then click a button (in this case the Format Painter), you're given a detailed explanation instead of the usual ScreenTip.
Press the Esc key to deactivate What's This?.

> **Format Painter (Standard toolbar)**
>
> Copies the format from a selected object or text and applies it to the object or text you click. To copy the
>
> formatting to more than one item, double-click ✎, and then click each item you want to format. When
>
> you are finished, press ESC or click ✎ again to turn off the **Format Painter.**

You can even get help from within a dialog box. Click the question mark at the top right of the title bar and a question mark appears beside your mouse pointer.

Now click an object (button, box, check box, etc.) and you will be given the information you 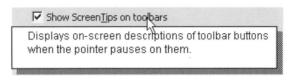 require. Any mouse click causes the explanation to disappear.

 You can achieve the same effect by clicking a dialog box object with the right mouse button. What's This? will appear at the pointer location in the form of a button. Click this to get a definition.

 You can still call upon the services of your trusty Assistant even when you've got a dialog box open, provided that your Assistant is already active.

Chapter 1

With which keys can you activate the menu bar?

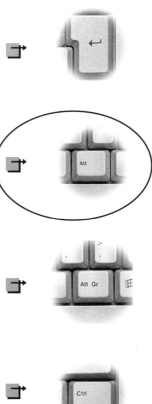

Which command sequence switches on ScreenTips?

➤ Format/Draw/ScreenTips

(➤) View/Toolbars/Customize/ScreenTips tab

➤ View/Toolbars/Customize/Options tab/ScreenTips on toolbars

What does your mouse pointer look like when it's in the document window?

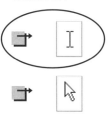

What is the purpose of the end-of-document marker?

➤ Text can be entered at the end-of-document marker's position

(➤) It indicates the end of the document.

➤ It marks the end of a sentence.

343

The sy-lla-ble ri-ddle

Use the syllables to form the correct answers. Four syllables will be left over to give the answer to the riddle.

Syllables: sta-text-pro-zoom-ker-mouse-tips-end-op-tus-view-mar-tabs-word-bar-screen-cess-tions-of-ing

Status bar

You will find information here, e.g. which page of the document you are on at the moment.

Zoom

You use this to enlarge or reduce the view of your document.

Mouse

Indicator and input device.

ScreenTips

If the mouse pointer stays on a button for more than a second, the explanation of that button appears.

End-of-text marker

Shows the end of a document.

Options

You switch on ScreenTips by clicking the View menu, choosing Customize from the Toolbars submenu, then clicking the .... tab to reveal the check boxes.

View

You use the .... menu to activate the ruler.

Tabs

They have 'index labels' (with the appropriate name on) which are used to bring them to the foreground.

The answer to the riddle is: __Word processing__

Chapter 2

Exercise 1

Are the following statements (t)rue or (f)alse?

(f)   If you accept the word 'human', you will correct all words which are spelled incorrectly.

(t)   If you select Add, the mistake will be ignored in all future documents.

(f)   If you select Ignore All, the mistake will be ignored in all future documents.

As an alternative to carrying out menu commands or clicking buttons, you can issue the same commands in Word using shortcut keys. Once you know them, the rest is EASY. Here are the most useful ones:

Command name	Key combination
Align left	`Ctrl` + `L`
Align right	`Ctrl` + `R`
All letters as capitals	`Ctrl` + `⇧` + `A`
Beginning of column	`Alt` + `Page↑`
Beginning of document	`Ctrl` + `Home`
Beginning of line	`Home`
Beginning of table line	`Alt` + `Home`
Bold	`Ctrl` + `B`
Bold	`Ctrl` + `⇧` + `B`
Bookmark	`Ctrl` + `⇧` + `F5`
Cancel	`Esc`
Center	`Ctrl` + `E`

Command name	Key combination
Change upper/lower case	⇧ + F3
Character format	Ctrl + D
Character left	←
Character right	→
Choose point size	Ctrl + ⇧ + P
Close document	Ctrl + F4
Column break	Ctrl + ⇧ + ↵
Copy	Ctrl + C
Copy	Ctrl + Insert
Cut	Ctrl + X
Decrease font size by 1 point	Ctrl + [
Decrease selection	⇧ + F8
Delete	Delete
Delete last word	Ctrl + ⌫
Delete word	Ctrl + Delete
Double underline	Ctrl + ⇧ + D
Double-space lines	Ctrl + 2
End of column	Alt + Page↓
End of document	Ctrl + End
End of line	End
End of table line	Alt + End
End of window	Alt + Ctrl + Page↓
Exit	Alt + F4
Extend character left	⇧ + ←
Extend character right	⇧ + →

Command name	Key combination
Extend line above	`⇧` + `↑`
Extend line below	`⇧` + `↓`
Extend selection	`F8`
Extend word left	`Ctrl` + `⇧` + `←`
Field codes	`Alt` + `F9`
Find	`Ctrl` + `F`
Font	`Ctrl` + `⇧` + `F`
Go to	`F5`
Help	`F1`
Help button	`⇧` + `F1`
Hidden	`Ctrl` + `⇧` + `H`
Increase font size by 1 point	`Ctrl` + `]`
Insert footnote now	`Alt` + `Ctrl` + `F`
Italic	`Ctrl` + `⇧` + `I`
Line above	`↑`
Line below	`↓`
Move document	`Ctrl` + `F7`
New	`Ctrl` + `N`
Next cell	`⇄`
Next spelling mistake	`Alt` + `F7`
Open	`Ctrl` + `O`
Page Break	`Ctrl` + `↵`
Page Layout View	`Alt` + `Ctrl` + `P`
Paste	`Ctrl` + `V`
Paste	`⇧` + `Insert`

Command name	Key combination
Print	`Ctrl` + `P`
Print Preview	`Ctrl` + `F2`
Repeat	`F4`
Repeat	`Alt` + `←—`
Replace	`Ctrl` + `H`
Restore document	`Ctrl` + `F5`
Save	`Ctrl` + `S`
Save	`⇧` + `F12`
Save As	`F12`
Select all	`Ctrl` + `A`
Select vertical block of text	`Ctrl` + `⇧` + `F8` then use arrow keys
Set 1.5-line spacing	`Ctrl` + `5`
Single-space lines	`Ctrl` + `1`
Small capitals	`Ctrl` + `⇧` + `K`
Split document window	`Alt` + `Ctrl` + `S`
Subscript	`Ctrl` + `=`
Superscript	`Ctrl` + `⇧` + `+`
Thesaurus	`⇧` + `F7`
Underline	`Ctrl` + `⇧` + `U`
Underline word	`Ctrl` + `⇧` + `W`
Undo	`Ctrl` + `Z`
Word left	`Ctrl` + `←`
Word right	`Ctrl` + `→`

349

What is each key for?

The [Alt] key

Short for 'Alternate Key', this is used for activating the menu bar in Windows programs. The [Alt] key also frequently plays an important part in shortcut key combinations.

The [⇧] key

The largest part of the keyboard is taken up by an arrangement that looks almost identical to that of a typewriter keyboard. Here you find almost the same functions that you know from a typewriter. For example, there is the [⇧] key (= Shift key). You use this to capitalise individual letters. First press the [⇧] key, hold it down, then type the required letter.

Example:

Above the number 5 in the row of numbers is the % sign. Hold down the [⇧] key and type 5. The % sign appears.

All the characters that appear above another character on the keys are typed in like this.

Type: 'A & O Ltd'

Further typing exercises:

£36

12 @ $4 each

15+3=18

Asterix Volume XXVII

5>4

Caps Lock Caps Lock

ALL LETTERS ARE WRITTEN IN CAPITALS WITH THIS KEY

Hint: The Caps Lock light comes on at the top right of the keyboard.

To cancel, press the Caps Lock key.

On some keyboards you'll find a third character assigned to various keys. You can type these by holding down the Alt Gr key at the same time. Even if there's no third character visible on the key top, the Alt Gr key can produce symbols, for example:

Alt Gr +c gives the copyright symbol (c),

Alt Gr +r gives the registered symbol (r), and

Alt Gr +t gives the trademark symbol (tm).

The ← key (Return key)

The ← key is another important key. You use it to tell the computer to start processing the command that you have just given it.

The Space bar

Press this key once to type a space between words.

The ⌫ key

Let's say you want to type the word 'mistake'.

You type

Mit_	and realise that you have done it wrong.
	You then press the ⌫ key.
Mi_	The 't' disappears.
Mistake_	Now you can type the word in correctly.

The numeric keypad

On the right-hand side of the keyboard is the numeric keypad.

Use the Num key to switch it on and off. If it's on, the Num Lock light automatically comes on.

The numeric keypad is very useful if you're just typing in numbers.

The cursor keys ← ↓ → ↑

Between the typewriter keyboard and the numeric keypad are the cursor keys. Use these to move the cursor about on the screen.

The function keys

Above the typewriter keyboard are the function keys F1 to F12. These do not produce any characters on the screen, but trigger a function or a process. The program currently in use determines what function the keys have.

Insert mode

As you type in words that you have omitted into the middle of a sentence, the rest of the text is moved along to the right. This mode is switched on and off using the Insert key.

Overwrite mode

Newly typed characters are written over the top of existing characters. This mode is switched on and off using the Insert key.

Keyboard summary

Function	Key cap
Depends on the program	`Alt`
Third character on keys	`Alt Gr`
Deletes the last character typed	`⌫`
Next screen	`Page ↓`
Previous screen	`Page ↑`
All capitals	`Caps Lock`
Move the cursor	`←` `→` `↓` `↑`
Sends the contents of the screen to the printer	`Print`
Inserts a character to the right of the cursor	`Insert`
Cursor jumps to end of line	`End`
Deletes a character to the right of the cursor	`Delete`
Interrupts the current action	`Esc`
Trigger a function or a process	`F1` to `F12`
Activates the numeric keypad	`Num`
Freezes the screen	`Pause`
The cursor jumps to the beginning of the line	`Home`
Command input	`↵`
Individual capital letters	`⇧`
Types spaces	`Space`
Depends on the program, in combination with another key	`Ctrl`
Causes the cursor to make a defined jump	`⇄`

353

AutoText Frequently recurring words and phrases can be stored as AutoText entries. These can then be called up in different documents by, for example, an abbreviation and the F3 key.

Browser Browsers are special applications that display information from the Internet and Internet hyperlinks on your screen. This software often comes pre-installed on your machine, or is supplied by your Internet Service Provider. However, it can also be obtained directly on the Internet. Microsoft Internet Explorer and Netscape Navigator are two of the standard browsers.

Cell Term for a field in a table.

Clip Art Word has a small library of ready-to-use images known as the Clip Gallery.

Clipboard In order to cut and paste text from one place in a document to another, and also to copy it, Windows generally uses the clipboard (a kind of temporary memory). Text is sent to the clipboard by the Copy or Cut commands. It can be inserted again where required (using the Insert command).

Combo-box In a combo-box you can choose from a list of values, or enter a new value of your own (such as font or font size).

Context menu If the right mouse button is pressed, a context menu opens. In a context menu, the options depend upon the situation in which the mouse key is pressed.

Cursor Indicates your position on the screen with a flashing vertical line. This marks the place at which your next input or instruction will appear.

Density The density of a floppy disk determines how much data it can hold.

Desktop The Windows 95 user interface on which the widows, icons and dialog boxes are displayed.

Directory Directories are like the drawers of a filing cabinet (= hard disk). All the files that belong together are stored in the same drawer (= directory). In Windows 95, directories are known as folders.

Document template A 'skeleton' document for frequently used documents such as letter heads or faxes. Templates can also hold macros and formats.

Double-click Two clicks in rapid succession with the mouse button.

DOT The file extension for Word document templates is '.dot'.

DPI Abbreviation for 'dots per inch', a measure of printer resolution.

Drag and drop A user interface procedure for transferring data from one place to aonther. This is a feature of Windows 95 and other similar graphical user interfaces. It allows you to move the mouse pointer to an object on the desktop, hold down the left mouse button to drag the object to another position, then drop it by releasing the button.

Dot matrix printer Every character printed is composed of a number of dots. Dots of ink are placed on the paper where the printer's needles hit an inked ribbon.

F1 Function key that activates Word's help facility.

File A collection of information stored together under a single name on a storage medium such as a hard disk.

File name A file name is composed of a meaningful name plus an extension. Word automatically supplies the extension '.doc' when you save documents.

File type Defines the type of file. In Word, you can choose between different types when you save a file (for example, with the extension '.txt') so that the file can be read by different programs.

Floppy disk write protection Floppy disks have a shutter that you can set to prevent them from being overwritten. If the little window at the bottom left of the disk is open, the disk can be read but the data stored on it cannot be overwritten.

Folder Area on a storage device that serves to organise the files saved onto it. Files can be stored here (see also directories).

Footnotes Explanations or further remarks on a particular text that are reproduced at the bottom of the page.

Formatting Determines the appearance of text on screen and when printed (using such effects as bold, italic, font).

Format template A set of formats that is grouped under a specific name with a document template.

Form letter A letter in which most of the text is the same. Only parts of it, such as the address or salutation, have to be changed for each recipient.

Gutter The gutter is an additional free area along the inner side of the page that is needed for binding loose sheets.

Header and footer These are the terms for text that is found inside the top or bottom margin of a page.

Hyphenation Automatic hyphenation breaks up words with hyphens during text entry when necessary, for example at the end of a line.

Icon Also referred to as a 'button' in Word. A symbol on the screen that stands for a computer function (such as the outline of a floppy disk for saving a file). An icon can also be used to control the course of a program (for example, the box file for opening a file).

Ink jet printer Printer that prints bt spraying ink onto the paper through nozzles at high pressure.

Italic The term for type that slopes slightly to the right.

Justified text Text that is aligned with both left and right margins. The spaces between the words are adjusted so that there is no ragged margin; either on the left or the right. Justified text can sometimes result in unattractively large gaps appearing in the text, especially if the line length is short.

Laser printer This type of printer works in a similar way to a photocopier. Individual dots on a roller are charged electrostatically in such a way that they attract toner (powdered ink). The toner is then pressed onto paper and bonded to it by heating.

Leaders Characters such as dots or dotted lines that fill the spaces between tabs.

Load Loading a file means the same thing as opening a file.

List box A list box offers you several entries to choose from. The entry chosen last remains displayed (such as in a format template).

Macro A sequence of commands that trigger actions and are processed one after the other when called.

Normal.dot Word's standard document template. It forms the basis of a new document and contains Word's standard settings for properties such as font, font size, button bars and key assignments. Changes have to be saved.

Numbered and bulleted lists Paragraphs can be made more eye-catching using bullets or automatic numbering.

Page break The place in a document at which one page ends and a new page begins (either inserted manually or automatically).

357

Pagination Term for page numbering.

Paragraph Continuous text that deals with a specific subject. Its first sentence starts on a new line. Often separated from previous and following text by a blank line. The ⏎ key in Word works in a similar way to a carriage return on a typewriter. A nonprinting character, the paragraph mark, is displayed.

Pica Measurement from typography, 1 Pica = 12 points (abbreviated pt), which corresponds to roughly 4.2mm.

Printer types The most popular types are ink jet printers, laser printers and dot matrix printers.

Proportional font A font in which each character has an individual print width.

Point A point is a traditional unit for the size of characters. A point corresponds to a character height of 0.35mm.

Ragged text Text with lines of different lengths, mostly with a straight left margin (the opposite of justified text).

RTF Abbreviation for Rich Text Format. A common transfer format which allows data to be exchanged between different programs. The Rich Text Format can be interpreted by other programs such as Word for Macintosh.

Ruler The calibrations that are visible at the upper edge of Word's working area.

ScreenTips Provide information about what is hidden behind Word's many buttons. If the mouse pointer remains for longer than a second on a button, an explanation is immediately displayed.

Scroll bar The strip on the edge of a document window that allows you to move quickly (scroll) through documents.

Shortcut A key combination that triggers a specific command.

Subscript Term for a character placed slightly below the line.

Superscript Term for a character placed slightly above the line.

Tab A tab set on the ruler (a left tab, right tab, decimal tab or centre tab) determines where the cursor will stop after the ⇥ key is pressed.

Tables Text and numbers are arranged in a table in rows and columns. The individual fields created by the intersections are called cells.

Thesaurus Greek term for a book of synonyms. In it you can look up words and find other words with the same or a similar meaning (example: 'building' instead of 'house').

TIFF Abbreviation for Tagged Image File Format, a graphics format.

Times Font that belongs to a large group of fonts called Baroque-Antiqua. Times is one of the most commonly used fonts.

True Type fonts Term for the screen and printer fonts used by Word.

Typography The art of composing type and printing from it.

Wildcard Characters that stand for part of a file name, and therefore enable a group of files to be listed together. The two most frequently used wildcards are '?' for a single character and '*' for multiple characters.

Wingdings With Windows 95, you get a TrueType font called Wingdings that contains a range of arrows and symbols.

WordArt MS WordArt is an application supplied with Word that allows you to create special font effects.

Zoom Word's Zoom function is used to enlarge or reduce the view of the current document.

light or dark? 281
move 251, 260, 315
rotate 261-2
sizing handles 315
sloping 261-2
text flow around 282
text in 262-7
as watermark 282
wrapping style 283
Greetings cards 267
Gridlines 146
Gutter 356

H

Header file 75
name 82
save 82, 92
Header row 76
Headers and footers 168-70, 270-1, 356
set 304
switching between 170
toolbar 168
Headings 51
in tables 96-7, 100-1, 133, 157-8
Help 335, 337
contents and index 339
in dialog box 340
ScreenTips 339
subjects 339
via the index 339
with icons 33
Hidden functions 176
Hyphenation 356-7

I

Icon 27, 179, 230, 324, 357
cancel 37
customise 326
definition 27
explanatory notes 27, 33
If ... Then ... If Not 87
Ignore all 106, 155
In Margin 303
Index
help 339
tab 22
Information zone 24, 28
Initial letters 305
Insert 179, 328
block 109, 112
calculated result 179, 184
columns 112
current date 152
field names 80, 84
mail merge fields 85
query conditional statements 87
rows 111
shading colour 129
special symbols 101, 102
tables 98
Insertion point indicator 24
Installation 335
Invitations 72, 75
Invoice, making out 168
Italics font 27, 52, 357

J

Justification 51, 357

365